MOORISH SPAIN

Cordoba Seville Granada

General Editors: Elizabeth and Paul Elek

Translation: Ian Michael

Production: Stanley Freeman

MOORISH SPAIN

Cordoba Seville Granada

Text by Enrique Sordo
Photographs by Wim Swaan

Elek Books 14 Great James Street London WC1

Published in Canada by
The Ryerson Press
299 Queen Street West
Toronto 2 B

Istituto Geografico De Agostini S.p.A. - Novara 1963 - Printed in Italy

TABLES OF CONTENTS

ACKNOWLEDGEMENTS

The publishers wish to express their gratitude to the directors of the Archaeological Museum at Cordoba and the Alhambra Museum, and to the Government and Municipal authorities in Cordoba, Granada and Seville for their kindness and co-operation.

Illustrations nos. 14, 24, 25 and 26 and the illustrations on *pp.* 46, 47, 76, 93, 107 and 109 of the text are reproduced by courtesy of the Victoria and Albert Museum.

The engravings on *pp.* 39, 140 and 210 are taken from the second edition of *Travels through Spain in the Years 1775 and 1776*, by Henry Swinburne, Esq., London, 1787.

The Genealogical Tables on *pp.* 56, 94 and 217 are taken from the *Encyclopaedia of Islam* by kind permission of the publishers, Luzac & Co., London, and E. J. Brill, Leiden.

LIST OF ILLUSTRATIONS

7

Plans and Tables

Inside front cover: Stone relief at the Palace of Medina Azzahra, Cordoba.

Inside back cover: Stucco work in *attawriq* designs on a wall in the Patio de los Arrayanes. Alhambra, Granada.

Binding Brass: Carved stucco motif on the wall of the Patio del Mexuar. Alhambra, Granada.

Jacket Illustrations:

Front: Patio de los Arrayanes, looking towards the latticed gallery of the Harem. Alhambra, Granada.

Back: Ceramic mosaic wall decoration in the Salón de los Embajadores. Alhambra, Granada.

ILLUSTRATIONS IN THE TEXT

INTRODUCTION

It is necessary to live for a time amid the subtle and exciting atmosphere that pervades the Arabic monuments of Cordoba, Seville and Granada in order to grasp the extent and importance of a very alien culture, many facets of which survive still. One must stroll along the streets and over the crossroads, enter the tiled dwellings and breathe the delicate fragrance of the Andalusian dusks and nights. One has to live among the people of Andalusia, eat their bread and drink their wine and hear them stoically consoling themselves when mishaps occur, with the words " we endured a greater loss in Granada," as though they tacitly consider themselves the heirs of the Arabs and African Moors who found their last refuge in that city. One needs to savour all these things and, at the same time, to search in ancient works and yellowed chronicles for the essential spirit of that unique and foreign world. As Lévi-Provençal tells us, " we must not shrink from the sudden intuitions that are sometimes triggered off in our minds by an unsuspecting study and a thorough knowledge of the original texts, nor should we turn away from the fleeting visions that an acquaintance with the early documents conjures up, for these texts will shed a great deal of light on the public and private life of that early period."

Western Islam, lying partly in Africa and partly in Europe, slowly emerges, during the Middle Ages, in its true colours, divested of the grey pall thrown over it by the unimaginative chroniclers, who were interested only in the various dynastic events. It becomes clear that, despite the vicissitudes of the centuries, throughout the whole of the Christian Conquest, the intellectual capital of the Moslem West always remained in Spain: first in Cordoba, then in several provincial cities, such as Seville, and finally in Granada. Whatever the state of its political fortunes, one can say that the land of al-Andalus never lost its spiritual sovereignty. Even when it was brought under direct Islamic rule by African monarchs, the land did not lose its power of attraction and soon captivated its new masters, who yielded to its delights and chose to settle in it permanently. A similar process took place later with the tough Castilian conquerors. On the latter as on the former Andalusia had the same effect as Greece had had on the Romans when it became part of their Empire. The words of the Latin poet are also relevant for Andalusia: *Graecia capta ferum victorem cepit* (" Vanquished Greece defeated its fierce conqueror ").

The essence of this land, which had a unique personality and which was able to absorb and invigorate the races and peoples that conquered it down the centuries, is distilled in three cities: Cordoba, Seville and Granada—cities that are very different from one another, although they have some features in common. Each has its own highly distinctive character, observable on the most hurried visit—which also reveals that they were cast in the same Arabic and Berber crucible: bustling Seville, now greatly changed by having become a large modern city and international tourist centre; Cordoba, quiet and captivating, where the eerily silent and fragrant streets evoke the Moorish *suks*, or markets, and the ghettoes of its finest period; Granada, the city of the Nasrid Sultans, magically Moorish even today.

Throughout the centuries men have attempted to define the unchanging characteristics of Andalusia. When the city of Cordoba decided to erect a monument in memory of its famous Bishop Hosius, who urged the summoning of the Nicene Council in 325, all the researches undertaken by the sculptor led him to the conclusion that the physical appearance of that cleric —tall, thin, sharp-featured, with large, dark eyes—was very similar to that of other famous men of Cordoba: Seneca the philosopher, the poet Lucan and the Great Captain, Gonzalo Fernández de Córdoba. Moreover, in the Homeric and prehistoric legends that tell of the myth of Hercules and of the paradise to be found in the land of Tarsis or Tartessos, we can discover characteristics very like those of present-day Andalusia. These characteristics are also found in descriptions by the Classical authors: in Pliny, when he describes the soil, the natural economy and the climate; in Strabo, when he tells of the fights with wild bulls; in Martial, when he talks of the supple, sensuous dances of Gades (Cadiz). All this evidence suggests that the successive invasions by alien races and peoples did not manage to obliterate the unchanging spirit of Andalusia; rather that spirit was enriched by them. Who would deny that of the various invasions the Moslem influx was most far-reaching in its effects? Furthermore, who would dispute that the Moslem influence, whether Arabic or Berber, is more manifest in Cordoba, Seville and Granada than elsewhere?

Cordoba seems to be immersed still in the warm atmosphere of Islam. The city centre and the suburb called the Judería (the Ghetto) are typically Moor-ish in plan. It is the daily life of Cordoba that appeals to us: a life full of tragic sense, silence and meditation, where the aristocracy and the people both preserve an air of gravity and seriousness. Whatever their social position, the inhabitants live in white-washed houses, most of which are built around a central *patio* or courtyard, furnished with a gurgling fountain, whitewashed archway, tiles, copper utensils, a palm-tree and above all flowers: jasmine, the tobacco-flower, sweet basil and a rose-bush. The clean, silent, narrow streets and secluded squares of Cordoba seem to be directly descended from a Moorish quarter.

Seville is different. Apart from the superb but tiny Barrio de Santa Cruz, a quarter with an air of neatness and balladry, and apart from the well-known Giralda, the Torre del Oro, the Puerta del Perdón, now much altered, and the Mudejar filigree-work of the Alcázar, few traces remain of the city's greatest period under Almoravid and Almohad rule.

But there is still Granada. If there exists in the Iberian Peninsula a city that epitomizes the essential Moorish spirit, without a doubt that city is Granada. That land between the Rivers Darro and Genil, the red walls and the gardens, the very character of the inhabitants, seem to encompass the history of Spain. From its foundation in primitive times Granada developed slowly, year by year, witnessing many changes and losing scarcely an iota of its peculiar character. This character was not formed purely by its natural advantages nor by the various phases and changes of its historical development, although these played an important role. Neither can it be attributed exclusively to the varied cultural influences that left their mark willy-nilly on its monuments, museums and streets, and on the daily lives of its inhabitants, though these influences, too, were important. But there was something else that constantly shaped and still shapes the fortunes of the people of Granada. This factor, which escapes the attention of archaeologists and art historians alike, consists of a very particular and immutable essential: the eternal spirit of Granada, independent of the invading influences that modified the city externally.

The ancient Spanish proverb, "everything is possible in Granada", is brought to life by one of the city's most famous historians, Gallego Burín, when he observes that Granada can offer everything, from the splendid remains of its lost Arabic culture to its odd corners of nineteenth-century Romanticism, from the extraordinary magic of Oriental art to the fervour of Gothic, from the vigour of the Renaissance to the almost excessive grandeur of Baroque. This impressive diversity should not be attributed only to the strangely blended artistry of the city, but also to the natural setting, which is full of surprising contrasts; in some places it is harsh and wild, in others delicate and subtle. Granada is neither a city of the mountains nor of the plain. Its contours are formed by a handsome intermingling of mountain and valley, offering a scene of outstanding interest and beauty. The mountains soar almost 10,000 feet above the plain, and they include the two highest peaks in Spain, the Veleta and the Mulhacén. It takes little more than an hour to descend from the peaks above the snow line to the temperate coast where tropical fruits flourish. Not for nothing did Granada's poet Federico García Lorca write of the Darro and the Genil:

> " Los dos ríos de Granada
> bajan de la nieve al trigo... "
> (" Granada's twin rivers flow
> down from the snow to the
> wheat... ").

CORDOBA

Cordoba.

Lejana y sola

García Lorca

CORDOBA

FOR A LONG PERIOD of history—three centuries in much of the country and eight centuries in the last Andalusian strongholds—Spain was almost completely dominated by the Moslems. This period, which was so momentous for the country's future development, began in the year 711 and ended in 1492, when Isabella of Castile and Ferdinand of Aragon brought the Reconquest to a conclusion with the military occupation of Granada, the last Mohammedan bulwark in the Peninsula. Even after this decisive rout, a large number of Moors remained settled in the country: these were the Moriscos, Moors who had been converted to Christianity and absorbed into the Christian population until their final expulsion in the seventeenth century under Philip III. Our interest, however, is drawn mainly to the first eight centuries of the Moors in Spain, for it was then that the real core of Moorish Spain was formed, especially in Andalusia, where so many and such diverse vestiges of Moorish, Arab and Berber influence persist. This period of eight centuries falls into several stages: 1. absolute Moorish ascendancy, with the establishment of Moorish sovereignty and way of life; 2. a counterpoise of the Moors and the Christians (i.e. Hispano-Romans and Visigoths), with a blending of their diverse elements; 3. ascendancy of the Christians and political disaster for the Moslems; 4. the continuing existence among the Spanish people of a Moslem proletariat consisting of Moriscos and Mudejars.

These four clearly defined stages correspond to equally distinguishable historical periods: the establishment of the Emirate dependent on Damascus; the independence of this Emirate and its rise in status to the Cordoban Caliphate; the political decline of the Caliphate, with a breaking-up of Arabic political unity into the so-called *taifa* (" faction ") kingdoms, one of which was Granada; and finally, occurring throughout these three periods, invasions by other North African tribes, the Almoravids (" the Devout Warriors ") and the Almohads (" the Unitarians "), who left many traces of their passage in Andalusia, and who fought not only the Christians of the Peninsula but also the members of their own race and religion already settled in the country. Another vital contribution to the fabric of Spanish culture at that time and to its continuance in later periods was provided by the large Jewish population. The Jews lived in both camps, Moslem and Christian; although they had more synagogues in the Christian areas, they played a much greater intellectual and cultural part among the Mohammedans than among the Christians.

The bewildering speed of the Moorish invasion and the conversion of many

Christians to the new religion put a new complexion on the problems that already confronted the Peninsula. In the few northern areas that escaped the Moslem yoke, the Visigothic tradition seemed to be providing the basis for a solution. In the South, that is to say in the greater part of the country, a fusion came about of the old Hispano-Roman traditions with those newly brought by the invaders, but the Moorish traditions dominated.

In some respects, of course, the Conquest was destructive. But the grandeur that the Eastern conquerors bestowed on Andalusia—their al-Andalus—cannot be denied. Although they were not the originators, as has often been affirmed, of the irrigation systems and the agricultural prosperity, they did improve and put the finishing touches to the work of the Romans by introducing new types of fruit and horticultural methods that were then virtually unknown outside Africa and Persia. In the same way, the Moors carried on and improved the Roman tradition of dwelling in fine cities. The present-day Moroccan *medinas* or townships, besides being a refuge for so many Andalusians, give an idea of what cities like Cordoba, Seville, Toledo, Almería and Granada were like in the tenth and eleventh centuries: craftsmen working in leather, metal, wood, pottery, and wool and silk weaving; merchants operating under a precise and complex municipal control; above all, the splendour of palaces, mosques, schools and libraries. All this occurred not only during the short-lived triumph of the Caliphate: al-Idrisi the geographer and Averroes the philosopher lived, not in the tenth, but in the twelfth century; at the end of that century the Giralda Tower was built in Seville, and the Alhambra Palace in Granada that has been so often considered a symbol of Hispano-Moslem civilization was really no more than a final glittering spark that rose in the fourteenth and fifteenth centuries.

It would be incomprehensible if no trace remained of this long and brilliant episode of Spanish history. Indeed, much has been said of the Arabic influences on the existing popular crafts like tapestry-making, pottery and so on, on music, on family customs, on the temperament and religious fanaticism of the Andalusian people. But this question must be treated warily. The term " Arabic " has the disadvantage of suggesting a racial influence that was actually more limited than is claimed. The Berbers, who were no strangers to the Peninsula, formed the largest part of the invading force, and much intermarriage rapidly brought about a relatively coherent " Hispano-Moorish " group. Moorish Spain was, in effect, a melting-pot in which elements from vastly different cultures were fused: evidence of this is provided by the Mosque at Cordoba and the Alhambra at Granada, which are harmonious but heterogeneous creations, built at the two extreme points of its evolution. The products of this crucible spread out towards Christian Europe and touched Scholastic Philosophy, Romanesque Art, the School of Medicine at Montpellier, the lyric poetry of the troubadours and the mystic poetry of Dante. This came about because the two worlds were not as separate as they might seem at first sight. There were wars, between the small Christian and Moorish groups, but there were also interchanges, intrigues, treaties and courteous relations. The rights of the conquered were soon guaranteed. Each society had its hierarchical pyramid. Among the Moslems, the Arab leaders, the soldiers, came first; then the Berbers; then the Christian renegades; and lastly the Mozarabs, Hispano-Romans who would not be converted to Islam. Among the Christians, the order was: the clergy and nobility; the Christian commoners who had not left Christian territory; the Mozarabs who had returned or been freed from Moorish rule; "new Christians" or converts; the Mudejars or Arabs

1. Door and blind arches in the western façade of the Mosque at Cordoba. A good example of the minute decoration in tile and bas-relief characteristic of the art of the Caliphate.

who lived in Christian territory but kept their own religion, customs and laws; the Jews, who were held in respect for a long period, and lastly the serfs. Culturally there was continuous interplay: there were Arabic-speaking Christians and Moslems who knew Latin and Romance; in Toledo and Seville were founded the most brilliant medieval centres of trilingual studies. In short, the Middle Ages saw a Spanish Islam full of a lively originality, whose wealth, thought and complexity prepared the ground, in no smaller measure than the Christian Reconquest, for the great fruition in the Spain of the future.

The Moslem conquerors of Spain were Arabs and North Africans. Their leaders were Arabs who brought with them the old tribal rivalries that had begun during Mohammed's lifetime and that were to continue in the Iberian Peninsula. This goes far in explaining the violent internal struggles that gripped the Spanish Arabic kingdoms for many centuries. The Visigothic political faction that supported Wittiza for the disputed throne desired and helped to bring about the Arabic invasion in the belief that after a satisfactory settlement the Arabs would return to the African territories they had subdued some years earlier. Not surprisingly, the outcome was rather different; for already in 710 there had been a successful, if minor, Moorish raid in search of plunder. Tarif, the leader of this raiding party, must have taken note of the weakness of the Visigothic State. In the following year his successor Tarik led into Spain an army consisting mainly of Berbers, some of whom were only recent converts to Islam; he probably had a reasonably good idea of his ultimate objective, otherwise, after he had won the first important battle of the Conquest on the River Guadalete, he would not have dared to make such a determined inland advance with an army of only 20,000 men.

Meanwhile the Hispano-Visigoths could not mount an adequate counter-attack because they had still not managed to integrate the two peoples that made up their community. This fact accounts for the series of rapid campaigns that enabled the Moorish leaders Tarik and Musa to conquer the whole of the Peninsula, from the Mediterranean to the Atlantic, except for a few Christian strongholds in the mountains and on the coasts of the North. As the Moors advanced, they obtained the submission of the big landowners who did not hesitate to come to terms or to apostatize in order to preserve their possessions. The labourers, too, perhaps because they understood little of Christianity, sought, by adopting the new creed, to escape from their bondage, which dated from the Roman Empire. This set of circumstances permitted the Moors to cross the Pyrenees, securing their line of retreat by creating vassal states, and to spread across the South of France as far as the Loire. Here, at Poitiers, one of the most decisive battles in history took place in 732 A.D., in which, for the first time in the West, the conquering thrust of Islam was checked.

The Moslems dominated the whole of the former Visigothic kingdom. After the defeat of Roderic, the last king of the Goths, at Guadalete, they went on with their task of taking over the territory, by force and by peaceful subjection. They compensated the Wittiza faction, which, being hostile to Roderic's followers, had facilitated the conquest, with grants of land. Many towns were allowed independent councils, since complete conquest, with garrisons everywhere, would have been impossible for an enemy rather lacking in numbers. Such an agreement was contracted between Abd al-Aziz, son of Musa, who was governor of al-Andalus until 716, and the Gothic Count Theodemir: he was granted a large area that was not clearly demarcated, between Valencia and Almería, with its centre at Orihuela; he would pay tributes but would enjoy internal freedom, subject

2. The eastern façade of the Cordoban Mosque, with triangular notched turreting and a series of doors with horse-shoe arches and coupled-arched windows alternating with buttresses.

always to the sovereignty of the Caliph. Pamplona, Lérida, Huesca, Barcelona, Gerona and Tortosa came under Moslem domination by similar means.

The Moors waged a "holy war" against those they called "polytheists" (Christians). They wanted to convert the world to Mohammed's doctrine, but as at that time Mohammedans were exempt from paying tax, a general conversion would have been inconvenient to the administration of the Caliphate. Since the government could not, for economic reasons, impose a religious tyranny that denied the native population the freedom to practise their own religion, agreements were contracted with important monasteries, and liberty to continue their former practices was granted to the original inhabitants of Seville, the see of Bishop Oppas of the Wittiza faction, and to those of Cordoba, where the Christians were allowed to continue worshipping in the old Cathedral of St Vincent, although they were not to disturb the Moslems with hymn-singing or bell-ringing. Thus a new social class arose: the Mozarabs, who were inferior to the Moslems and who were not permitted to employ them or surpass them in office or position. Although the Moslems' policy was to exclude Christians from administrative posts, their collaboration had to be sought in practice: the continuance of two legal systems required that the Christian leaders in many places should act as judges of their own people.

In the areas that Islam began to lose before the eighth century, no traces of their rule have survived: in Catalonia and on the Cantabrian coast there have been practically no Moorish finds; this seems to confirm that the Moslem occupation of these lands was entirely military, with no important consequences for the future. A sharp contrast can be observed to the south of an imaginary line marking off the area where the Arabization became much more intense. This southern area, which was almost completely Arabized, was called al-Andalus by the Moslems, and from this comes the name of present-day Andalusia. The etymology of the word is confused: apparently the Berbers in the fifth century called Spain *Tamurt Wandalus* ("Land of Vandals"). Possibly this name later became *Andalus*, preceded by the Arabic definite article *al*: al-Andalus.

The Arabs and Berbers who served in the ranks of the invading army were nomads (*Arab* means "nomad"), and they were not particular about settling in a definite place. They had no feeling for their native land and they raced on in search of glory, wealth and plunder wherever these could be found. They never hesitated to leave their new homes and press forward, for they had few chattels and all their ambitions were centred on possessing precious objects that were light in weight and animals that could follow them. Their esteem for moveable goods and cattle was imparted to many of the peoples with whom they came into contact, including those who were later to form the Spanish nation. Despite their nomadic instincts, the Arabs and North Africans who settled in Andalusia seemed to abandon their former outlook and become mesmerized by this land and determined to stay there for ever. The psychological reasons for this change are difficult to understand. It may have resulted from the climate and the natural surroundings which were kinder than in the lands of their origin. The fact is that it happened and that the Spanish Moslems became almost a race apart, especially in their most splendid period, during the Caliphate of Cordoba, and in the subsequent period of the *taifa* kingdoms, of which Granada was one of the most important.

The Cordoban Emirate, dependent on Damascus, lasted for more than forty years, until the accession in 755 of the Emir Abd al-Rahman, who was to break many ties with the central power of the vast Arab Empire. This man, destined to rule nearly the whole of Spain, was a Syrian from the Damascus region and belonged to the imperial Umayyad family. When his family lost the throne as a result of their fierce struggle with their rivals the Abbasids, Abd al-Rahman was forced to flee the country and reached Spain after undergoing many vicissitudes. There he overthrew the two men who held sway on behalf of the government of Islam, Yusuf and Ismail, and soon declared himself and the country independent of the Caliph of Baghdad, the then supreme ruler of the Moslem world. So there began in Spain a new Syrio-Arab dynasty, transferred to the West. Nearly the whole of the Peninsula was to have a single leader, whose authority, however, would be ceaselessly disputed. After putting down the anarchy in his kingdom, Abd al-Rahman had to remain in a constant state of military preparedness to defend his throne against the intrigues of the Yemenites, the Berbers and many other hostile sects and factions. The new emir had to suppress plots and revolts until his death. His very friends, and even those members of his own large family, the Umayyads, who were brought from Damascus or who came to Spain to benefit from their relative's good fortune, conspired against him. He was obliged to banish to Africa one of his brothers, al-Walid, whose son had hatched a plot. Al-Walid, appalled by his son's execution at Abd al-Rahman's command, vehemently protested his loyalty and obedience. But his brother's self-abasement did nothing to dispel the suspicions of the Emir, who observed to one of his entourage: " Let him have no hope of deceiving me. I know him well, and I know that if he had the opportunity to quench his vengeful thirst with my blood he would not hesitate to do so. " The Umayyad Emir became a tyrant; the ruler who had once been popular now dared not stroll through the streets of Cordoba, his capital and the heart of his dominions. Being uncertain of his personal security, he sent to Africa for Berbers to form his bodyguard, and increased the size of his escort to 40,000 warriors. His successors also considered it necessary to maintain the same large force. The Caliphate could not survive without becoming a sort of military dictatorship.

An Arab historian has described how eloquent and elegantly spoken Abd al-Rahman was and how, like all self-respecting Arabs, he was something of a poet. He is said to have been sharp-witted, well educated, with a generous though determined nature, always ready to persecute rebels and never wasting time in restful or leisurely pursuits. He never discussed his policies with anyone, always trusting in his own judgement. He was endowed with good intelligence and his almost rash courage was tempered by great discretion. He almost always dressed in white. Despite the qualities described by this contemporary historian, it is difficult now to judge the morality of the Emir's actions, which were no doubt forced on him by special circumstances and by the barbarous habits of both his enemies and his friends. He was obliged not only to defend his person but also the destiny of Islam in the West and became inured to fighting and behaved on many occasions in the same deceitful, perfidious and cruel way as his adversaries. But this colossal red-haired man seems also to have had a streak of barbarity in him, inherited no doubt from his nomadic Yemeni forbears. He did not stop at merely imposing terrible sentences but would himself carry them out: on one occasion he tried to stab a chieftain from Seville, against whom he held certain grievances; but the victim defended himself so successfully that Abd al-Rahman had to call his guards to despatch his opponent.

At the same time, it is clear that he had a high opinion of himself and his own greatness. He was no ordinary status seeker. He had brought with him from the East the concept of imperialism, which, after the fall of Rome and of the Visigothic Monarchy, had almost been forgotten in Spain and North Africa (*i.e.* the Maghrib). Abd al-Rahman cherished the dream of a new Western Empire, or at least a great monarchy based on autocratic principles. But the incessant wars he was obliged to wage prevented him from emerging as a great governor or as a renovator and constructor. He scarcely had time for construction in the true sense: he began work on the great Mosque at Cordoba and he adapted as best he could for his needs the *castellum* of the earlier Roman and Visigothic governors. He had to leave unrepaired the long bridge over the Guadalquivir, which had lost its arches during a flood. All he managed to complete was a country house at the foot of the spurs of the sierra on the outskirts of Cordoba. This house was called al-Rusafa after the palace which his grandfather Hisham had built in Damascus. In the meantime the invaders' blood had become mixed: Abd al-Rahman I, the founder of the dynasty, was the son of a Berber slave-girl; Abd al-Aziz, the son of Musa, the Conqueror of Spain, had married Egilon, King Roderic's widow. After this princess, a throng of female Christian captives and slaves entered the harem of the Moslem monarchs, among them the Sultana Aurora and the favourite al-Rumaikiya. This constant breeding with women of Berber, Iberian or Visigothic stock produced a line that had little that was Arab in it, though it was not purely Spanish either. Most of the caliphs were fair or ginger-haired with blue eyes, which seems to show a preponderance of Berber or Germanic blood. As they were extremely proud of their origin, some of them dyed their hair black, as if to affirm their Arab descent.

The first emirs, dedicated wholeheartedly to their forays, their family and tribal rivalries, and their wars of extermination, do not appear to have been much concerned with the comforts or the refinements of civilized life. It was not until the reign of Abd al-Rahman II (822-852) that the Spanish Moslems began to imitate the luxurious living of the Orient: " it was this sovereign," a chronicler tells us, " who first introduced the customs, which became normal in the Caliphate, of pomp and outward display, of an organized royal household and of wearing sumptuous apparel. His palaces were decorated and water supplies were installed in them... " He built mosques throughout Spain, he commanded that clothes should be adorned with embroidery and trimming and protected their manufacture; he founded the Mint (the *Ceca*) in Cordoba, and generally promoted the outward show of his royalty. During his reign, rich tapestries and other precious objects were brought to Spain from Baghdad and other Oriental cities. Abd al-Rahman II wanted not only to rival but to outdo the Court of the Abbasids at Baghdad. That Court had come under Persian influence and was a byword for elegance in the Moslem world. Abd al-Rahman therefore brought from Baghdad the famous musician Ziryab, to teach the Spaniards good tone, not only in music and poetry but also in fashions, clothes and manners. In spite of his efforts, Abd al-Rahman was unable to rid himself of the barbarous streak he had inherited.

The Andalusian climate, however, mellowed the descendants of these rough horsemen: soon they became sensual and pampered, fond of wine, singers and dancing-girls, and all the delights that had made Gades (Cadiz) and its women famous during the Roman Empire. It must be remembered that all this was forbidden by the law of the Prophet: the wine, the music, the dancing and even the hunt. The emirs had taken to hunting after the fashion of their predecessors, the Gothic Kings, and the other habits prohibited by the Koran naturally

3. The *mihrab* in the Mosque at Cordoba. An enclosed chamber of foiled arches which began to replace the earlier horse-shoe arches.

4

5

followed. In some cases, in music for example, their enthusiasm reached the state the Arabs call the *tarab*, which is the moment when spiritual emotion is experienced as physical pleasure. The great Arabist Emilio García Gómez has this to say of the *tarab*:

" With regard to the origin of this word, some suppose it to be from the root *taba*, meaning ' to experience pleasure '. As for its derivatives, Julián Ribera saw in it a possible etymon for the Spanish words *trovero* and *trovador* (' minstrel '), i.e. ' producers of *tarab* '; a very interesting suggestion, although Romance philologists are very reluctant to accept it.

" Arabic books are full of stories about the *tarab*. If any of them begin to tell us that a slave-girl who is a good singer has placed the lute on her lap, tuned its strings and started to sing an old song, we can be sure that further down on the page we shall be told that the listeners' ' soul has fled ', that they have fainted, fallen breathless to the ground, foamed at the mouth, slapped their own faces, torn their clothes or beaten their heads against the wall; not to mention the weeping and sighing that went on. A prisoner convicted of high treason sang before the Caliph al-Mamun, and one of the courtiers present was so moved that he kissed him, fully aware that such action might bring about his own death. The Caliph Yazid, enraptured by a singer, snatched up a cushion from his sofa, placed it on his head and ran dementedly about the room crying ' Fresh fish! '. There is an amusing anecdote of an event of this type that took place in Seville in the eighth century: a slave-girl singer arrived from the East and two enthusiastic citizens went to hear her at her master's house. The room was poorly furnished and the singer was ugly and dirty. But how she could sing! The visitors did somersaults over the divans and also imitated street-criers. One of them put on his head some bottles of olive-oil, which ran out and trickled over him. This slave-girl was later purchased by Abd al-Rahman I.

" The loss of this capacity for great physical emotion—even in its less violent forms—seems to me to show a present-day lack of sensitivity. If any trace of *tarab* remains, it must be sought at the bull-fight or other sporting events. It is greatly subdued in oratory, and almost non-existent in drama and poetry. But no; I am not telling the truth. Spain, that stronghold of ancient forces, still keeps the *tarab* in its *cante hondo*: an inner room in an Andalusian tavern; glasses of golden wine; a guitar; a voice... The *olé* of the *cante hondo* is still the *wallah* (' oh God ') with which the Arabs cheered every poetic recitation."

All the independent Cordoban caliphs that followed Abd al-Rahman II seem to merge into a pattern of almost complete impersonality, despite their many political reforms and military conquests both of the Christians and of their own internal enemies. Up to the time of the disintegration of the Caliphate, only two monarchs emerge by their greatness and power: Abd al-Rahman III, the Great, under whose rule Cordoba became a truly imperial capital, and al-Mansur, the usurper, who attained power by every kind of crime and intrigue, soon holding the whole of Spain in the palm of his hand.

During the long reign of Abd al-Rahman III (912-961) the wars were nearly continuous, just as in the earlier reigns. The fifty years of this Caliph's rule were filled with struggles against the Arab aristocracy, the renegade Spaniards, the Christians within his territory and without, and lastly, the Fatimid Sect from the Maghrib. By means of astuteness and at times by treachery, by his relentless and cruel severity and above all by his unbreakable resolution, Abd al-Rahman III managed to be respected by most of his enemies and to establish almost absolute

4. Fourteenth-century cupola in the Chapel Royal in the Cordoban Mosque. There is no Granada *mocárabe* decoration in this chapel, but the influence of Mudejar and Nasrid art is clearly visible, especially in the large number of foiled arches, of Eastern origin, which are not found in the art of the Caliphate.

5. Detail of the mosaics on the walls of the *mihrab* in the Mosque at Cordoba. The colouring and delicacy of the decoration are characteristic of the handiwork of the craftsmen whom al-Haquem II obtained from Byzantium.

27

authority in al-Andalus, or Moslem Spain. But his achievement was ephemeral for two main reasons: first, because it was virtually impossible to impose obedience on peoples so unruly and disinclined to bear any kind of yoke; secondly, because the wars were never properly concluded, either for lack of men or money, or as a result of a nomadic convention of war: in the classical *algazúa* or foray, the army turned back when sufficient booty had been obtained. In practice, this booty included some prisoners and a few heads which were then placed on spikes on the bridge at Cordoba. The caliphs considered it enough that there should be a no man's land between the Moors and Christians, and to create it they destroyed crops and groves, and burned and sacked villages, leaving a belt of completely bare country.

Medina Azzahra

The most lasting achievement of Abd al-Rahman the Great was his architecture. Like many other warriors, he was a great builder, as though new construction would obliterate for him the memory of old destruction. He adorned and extended the old palace in Cordoba. He erected the minaret of the Great Mosque and rebuilt the façade of the mosque itself over the front of the old Christian Church of St Vincent. But he lavished most care on Medina Azzahra, which was partly a fortress and partly a country house, and was much admired by Arab writers. Apparently he built this country mansion to please his favourite Azzahra, who begged him to bestow her name on that magical palace. This building, intended partly for pleasure and partly for defence, appears as a symbol of the evolution of the Moslem monarchs: their story of violence and lust, which gradually lost its epic character and became hedonistic and sceptical in outlook.

The Arab chroniclers have left us an account of the history and a description of the legendary city of Azzahra: it was long thought that they had exaggerated its magnificence, but recent excavations have fully confirmed their accounts (*ill.* 22). The building took forty years, though the main part was finished in fifteen. It was begun by Abd al-Rahman III and continued by his son al-Haquem II, but the work was interrupted on the latter's death. The site chosen lay on the outskirts of Cordoba, on the lower slopes of the Sierra Morena, and measured 1660 yards long by 815 yards wide, making a total area of almost 280 acres. The land was divided into three descending terraces, each terrace surrounded by turreted walls that gave it the false appearance of a fortress. On the upper terrace stood the Caliph's palace and a line of fine forts; the middle terrace consisted of shaded gardens and a game reserve; the lower terrace contained the living quarters of slaves and servants, and the great mosque. This mosque and the reception room overlooked the River Guadalquivir. According to the chroniclers, the construction involved between ten and twelve thousand workmen, the transport of the materials being provided by fifteen thousand mules and five thousand camels. The marble was brought from Carthage and Tunis. The decoration consisted of quite simple geometric designs, mainly circular or oval medallions, similar to those found in Byzantine and primitive Moslem art. Most of the very beautiful decorative motifs were floral, based on the leaves of the acanthus and the vine, but abstractly represented. Their simple beauty and harmony bear a strong resemblance to motifs in Greek art and a much weaker resemblance to Islamic artistic traditions. Their only Eastern model may have been in Byzantine art, and this is understandable if we remember that the caliphs sent to Byzantium for sculptors and mosaicists.

The Arab historians describe the city of Medina Azzahra in tones of wonder and rapture. Al-Makkari tells us that it was situated between the mountains and the plain that stretches as far as Cordoba, at about three miles from the city outskirts. It was one of the most splendid constructions ever undertaken by mankind. It contained 4,300 pillars and 500 doorways, and cost an enormous amount of money to build. It is known that the annual revenues of al-Andalus at that time amounted to 5,480,000 *dinars* from general taxation, 765,000 *dinars* from the market-taxes, a fifth of all the booty captured from the enemy, and the tributes paid by Jews and Christians. Of these revenues, the Caliph allotted one third to paying the army, another third to the royal treasury for household expenditure, and the remainder to the construction of Medina Azzahra and the other new buildings undertaken in his reign.

Ibn Hayyan provides a detailed account of the building costs of the palace and city of Medina Azzahra. The work began in the year 325 of the Hegira (936-37 A.D.) and continued during the following forty years, the first twenty-five in the reign of Abd al-Rahman III, and the remainder in that of his successor al-Haquem II. The main part of the palace was completed well before Abd al-Rahman's death, but his son al-Haquem made many additions such as the court reception-rooms, the military barracks, the pleasure-gardens, the baths and the fountains. In Abd al-Rahman's time, the building operations required each day 6,000 blocks of stone, some polished and others rough, of all shapes and sizes, not counting the special stones used for paving and other purposes. These materials were transported by 400 animals; some accounts claim that, in addition to the Caliph's 400 camels, 1,000 mules were hired at a cost of three *mizcales* per month each, making a monthly total of 3,000 *mizcales*. Every three days, 1,100 loads of clay and plaster were used up. The total number of various-sized pillars constructed was 4,000; again, other accounts make this figure 4,316. Of these, some were brought from Rome, nineteen came from the Frankish Kingdom, 140 were presented by the Emperor of Constantinople, 113, mostly of pink or green marble, were imported from Carthage, Tunis, Sfax and other places in North Africa. The remainder came from Spanish quarries: those at Tarragona and Almería provided columns of white marble. We are also informed that, for each block of marble, large or small, that was carried to Cordoba, the Caliph paid ten gold *dinars*. A palace servant asserted that the total annual cost of building Medina Azzahra was 3,000,000 *dinars*.

The palace had 1,500 doors, counting each leaf separately, and they all had iron facings dressed with burnished bronze. Ibn Hayyan tells us that among the wonders of the city were two fountains that were as extraordinary in shape as they were magnificent in workmanship, and in his opinion they constituted the palace's most important ornaments. The larger fountain was made of gilt bronze and was wonderfully sculpted with bas-reliefs of human figures. It had been brought to the Caliph from Constantinople. The smaller fountain was of green marble and had come from Syria, although some historians claim that it, too, was brought from Constantinople. All are agreed, however, on the magnificence of its material and workmanship. It reached al-Andalus by ship, and when the Caliph received it he had it placed either in an alcove in the Salón de los Califas or in the *patio* called al-Munis, and surrounded it with twelve pieces of statuary, made of red gold and set with pearls and other gems. The figures were made in the workshops of Cordoba and they represented lions, stags and crocodiles on one side of the fountain, an eagle and a dragon on the other, and at the ends there were a dove, a falcon, a duck, a hen, a cockerel, a kite and a vulture. All these animal figures were adorned with jewels and emitted water from their mouths.

Another of the marvels of Medina Azzahra was the Salón de los Califas, which had a ceiling and walls made of gold and multi-coloured, translucent marble blocks. In the centre of this hall, and according to some accounts set above the fountain we have just described, was the unique pearl which had been presented to the Caliph, together with other precious objects, by the Emperor Leo. The drapings in this magnificent room were made of gold and silver, and some say that its centre-piece was a large pool filled with quicksilver. On each side of the hall were eight doors decorated with gold and ebony, which stood between piers of coloured marble and clear crystal. When the sun shone into the room and reflected on the walls and roof, it produced a blinding effect. When the Caliph wished to astonish his visitors, he would signal to one of the slaves to disturb the pool of quicksilver; at once the hall would be filled with flashes of light and those gathered would begin to tremble because, so long as the mercury quivered, the

Tile and stucco decoration on the wall of the Mosque at Cordoba.

Stucco wall decoration.

whole room appeared to revolve around a central axis following the movement
of the sun. There was an abundance of mercury in Spain, and Abd al-Rahman
himself had designed this *trompe-l'oeil*, entrusting its secret only to his son al-Haquem.
Although their accounts differ in several details, all the chroniclers were unani-
mous in asserting that the splendour of this hall had never been equalled.

The mosque at Medina Azzahra was worthy of the rest of the palace. Despite
its incomparable design and proportions, it was completed in forty-eight days;
Abd al-Rahman put to work 1,000 skilled workmen, of whom 300 were masons,
200 carpenters and the remainder bricklayers and men of other trades. It was
a magnificent structure, consisting of five finely-wrought naves. The courtyard
was completely paved in wine-coloured marble. In the centre was a fountain
of limpid water for use in the mosque. The main nave was richly decorated,
and the Caliph ordered an extremely fine pulpit to be placed in it on the day
the mosque was completed, in the 329th year of the Hegira (23rd January, 941
A.D.). On that day, which other historians say was the 22nd and a Friday, public

prayers were said for the first time in great solemnity; the Caliph attended and the Cadi Abu Abd Allah ben Abi Isa officiated as imam.

In Medina Azzahra there were two baths, one for the Caliph's household and the other for the public; in addition, there were markets, inns, colleges and other institutions. The opulent gardens had many streams and water-courses, and there were fine houses for the court officials and the large crowd of pages, slaves and eunuchs who filled the city. The total number of male palace-servants is said to have been 13,750, and this great number was fed each day with 13,000 pounds of meat, not counting poultry and fish. There were also 3,350 (some say, 3,387) slaves and eunuchs. A surprising innovation, which was to remain undiscovered in the rest of Europe for centuries, was the installation of running water in the city's latrines. The palace's fish-tanks were supplied each day with 12,000 loaves of bread and six *cahices* (about 115 bushels) of black seeds.

With its marble-paved terrace overlooking the fine gardens, the magnificent decoration of the golden hall and the circular pavilion, its artifical lake and its reservoir always filled with clear water, Medina Azzahra must have been a dream-palace indeed.

The City of Cordoba

Sánchez Albornoz asserts that Cordoba's population had reached a total of half a million in the time of Abd al-Rahman III, that is to say, in the first half of the tenth century. The number of its inhabitants went on increasing until the internal revolts that began in 1009. It included a growing Christian element, a considerable Jewish population, and from al-Mansur's time a number of Berbers. As well as being numerous, the Cordobans were turbulent and pleasure-loving; but there was amongst them a powerful aristocracy who imitated al-Haquem II in building up libraries and in generally fostering learning and the arts. The city was bureaucratic, cultured and commercial at the same time. It formed the centre of the great Umayyad Empire and housed all the institutions of court and government. Under the patronage of the Caliph and the magnates, a large group of learned men lived in Cordoba: physicians, philosophers, writers, historians, geographers, astronomers and mathematicians.

The names of some of Cordoba's principal thoroughfares and suburbs—Pergamineros, Perfumistas, Zapateros, Silleros, to name but a few— reveal its once flourishing industries: parchment, perfumes, shoes, saddles. Markets were set up for trade in books, slaves, cereals (one year there was too good a harvest and wheat had to be burned to prevent a drop in prices) and many other commodities. There was barter in hides from Saragossa, pottery from Calatayud, weapons from Toledo, carpets from Cuenca, silks from Valencia and Granada, leather and tapestries from Cordoba itself. These markets also saw extremely varied objects of luxury and exotic merchandise that entered al-Andalus through the seaport of Pechina, near Almería. John of Görz, ambassador of Otto I, expressed his amazement at the splendour of Cordoba under the caliphs in his description of his embassy to Abd al-Rahman III. News of the grandeur of the capital of Moslem Spain even reached a quiet cloister in Saxony, where the nun Hrotsvitha of Gandersheim called it " the world's ornament ".

Like Byzantium, which it resembled more closely than it did the purely Oriental city of Baghdad, Cordoba stood at the crossroads of East and West. At a time when Europe had reached the lowest living standards it had ever known, the

6. The red-and-white striped arches of the Cordoban Mosque.

7. The arches and columns of jasper, marble and other fine stone of the earliest part of the Cordoban Mosque: the twelve naves built by Abd al-Rahman I.

city on the Guadalquivir, like the city on the Bosphorus, kept the torch of civilization ablaze. As we have said, the vast majority of the inhabitants of al-Andalus were of Spanish origin, and the best brains of those living in Cordoba were intellectually enriched by Arabic thought and knowledge, producing the greatest cultural flowering Spain was to experience until its Golden Age in the seventeenth century. That early flowering was to ripen in the following century, at the time of the *taifa* kingdoms.

Various historians give different accounts of the size of Cordoba during the Caliphate, presumably because of the speed with which the city expanded and the difficulties of making such estimates. Al-Shakundi tells us that the city, including Medina Azzahra, was ten miles long and at night, he adds, lanterns were necessary to light the way. The circumference of the city walls was estimated to be seven and a half miles. The city was said to be over two miles broad from north to south, not counting the outer suburbs. Another account claims that Cordoba was extended under the Umayyad Dynasty to twenty-four miles in length and six miles in width—all this area along the banks of the Guadalquivir being covered with palaces, mosques, gardens and houses.

Cordoba has been described as the city that, from the moment of its occupation by the Mohammedans, steadily increased in size, population and splendour until the 400th year of the Hegira (1009-10 A.D.) when civil war broke out. Thereafter it was stripped of its former power and grandeur. It continued declining until its final destruction in 1236 A.D. when it was captured by the Christians.

Some historians estimate the area covered by Cordoba, including the outer suburbs, at about fifty-one square miles, of which almost two squares miles were taken up by royal palaces. Yet another historian asserts that the city was divided into five large districts, separated from one another by turreted walls, and that the total area measured three miles long by one mile wide. It has also been claimed that there was a total of twenty-one suburbs, each of which had its own public markets, mosques and baths. These suburbs had evocative and delightful names: the Jardín de las Maravillas (Garden of Wonders), the Tiendas de los Vendedores de Albahaca Dulce (Shops of the sweet-basil sellers), the Arrabal de los Panaderos (Bakers' Quarter), the Mezquita del Regocijo (Mosque of the Rejoicing) etc. In the city centre stood the Alcazaba, a high-walled fortress.

One chronicler, describing the royal palace in Cordoba, says that it was an old building once inhabited by the " infidel sultans who ruled the land from the time of Moses ". Like the buildings that surrounded it, it contained fine remains of the earlier structures of the Greeks, Romans, Goths and other nations that had by then passed into oblivion. The rooms were beautifully decorated and full of enchanting ornaments. The first caliphs took over this palace as their residence and enlarged and embellished it. They also improved the city by providing delightful gardens, water from the Sierra de Córdoba and a sound economy. The mountain water was channelled to the palace, and from there it ran to all the city suburbs through lead pipes, which emptied into basins of all shapes and sizes, some made of fine gold, others of silver or silver-plated copper, and into large pools and reservoirs, as well as handsomely wrought fountains of Greek marble. In the palace there was an amazing water-jet, which shot the water to a considerable height—a type of fountain commonly found in the East.

It is not known who built this palace originally, but the general opinion was that it was constructed by an early king who lived in the fortress of Almodóvar. The legend goes as follows:

8. Stone lattice and foiled arch in the Mosque at Cordoba, with characteristic arabesques of stylized floral motifs.

37

" One day, when the king was out hunting, he approached the spot where Cordoba was later to be built, it being then a desert. The site later occupied by the Alcázar was covered in thick undergrowth. Nearby the king released his favourite falcon, which flew over the field in search of a partridge. The king lost sight of it and, fearing that it had become entangled in the brambles, he ordered the bushes to be scythed down so that it could be freed. While his followers were engaged in this task, they discovered the top of a fine building, which had been amazingly constructed with large blocks of stone, joined together with molten lead. The king, who was both intelligent and enterprising, ordered an immediate excavation and the whole building was soon revealed. The king then commanded that the great palace should be restored and made habitable. Thenceforth he visited it at intervals as he did his other palaces. The result was that many of his subjects settled in the neighbourhood, thus forming the city of Cordoba, with the palace still at its centre. "

Of the palace doors dating from the Moslem period—doors that " all-powerful Allah opened to help the oppressed, to redress grievances and to dispense impartial justice in all lawsuits "—the main doorway had a balcony which, according to one chronicler, was without equal. This entrance consisted of folding doors, faced in iron and secured by a copper adornment representing an open-mouthed man, which also served as a door-knocker and which had originally belonged to the French city of Narbonne. Another of the doors was called the Mosque Door, because the early caliphs used it to go to the Great Mosque on Fridays, when the whole route was carpeted in their honour.

In addition to the royal palace, the emirs and caliphs of the first Moslem dynasties had built several houses and gardens in Cordoba and in the surrounding countryside. Many of the gardens belonging to the caliphs and magnates were open to the populace for rest and enjoyment. The most famous of these was the garden of the al-Rusafa Palace, which had been built by Abd al-Rahman I and became his favourite residence. The garden was filled with exotic trees and plants and was well irrigated. That monarch's horticultural enthusiasm led him to send to Syria and other distant lands for all kinds of seeds, which were then nurtured in the palace gardens and later distributed throughout al-Andalus. From these gardens came the *safari* pomegranates, which we are told had incomparable flavour and succulence.

The Palace of al-Rusafa stood to the north of Cordoba and was named after the *al-kasr* that Abd al-Rahman's grandfather had built in Damascus. In addition to this royal residence, there were many other palaces in Cordoba and the surrounding area, some of which were famous: the Palacio del Confluente, the Palacio del Jardín, the Flores, the Enamorado, the Afortunado etc. The most renowned was the Dimashk: its roofs were supported by tall marble columns and its floors paved in multi-coloured mosaics. It was also famous for its sweet-smelling gardens, filled with flowers and fruit, with fine perspectives and clear streams.

In the vicinity of Cordoba there were no less than 3,000 towns, all with mosques and *musallas* or religious courts. All the *cadis* of these towns were obliged to accompany the Caliph to the Mosque at Cordoba on Fridays. After the religious service, they would in turn give the Caliph an account of the affairs of their areas. A usually reliable writer, who lived in Cordoba in al-Mansur's time, tells us:

" I once counted all the houses in the city and the suburbs and found that they came to a total of 213,077; this figure includes the dwellings of the common people

38

Chapel of the Alkoran in the Mosque of Cordoba. Engraving by F. Giomignani from a drawing by Henry Swinburne; 1776.

such as workmen and artisans, but excludes the rented attics, inns, baths and taverns. The palaces of the nobles, viziers, officials of the royal household, generals and wealthy citizens, the barracks, hospitals, colleges and other public buildings come to a total of 60,300."

The same author estimates the number of business premises at 80,455.

Detail of original Moorish door in the Court of the Maidens at the Alcázar in Seville.

Among the most famous constructions undertaken by Abd al-Rahman III was the famous Mosque at Cordoba. He did not build the whole structure, since it had been begun by his ancestors. From the year 748 A. D., the old Visigothic Church of St Vincent had provided a place of worship for both the Mozarab Christians and the Moslems. In 785, Abd al-Rahman I purchased from the Mozarabs their part of the church and in twelve months built the Mosque over it. Because of the urgency with which it was erected, many features of the earlier basilica were retained. In the building as it stands today, the part constructed by Abd al-Rahman I comprises the northwest corner of the Hall of Prayers. Its lay-out departs radically from that traditionally employed in Oriental mosques, partly because of the utilization of the plan and other features of the Visigothic church. In contrast to the usual spacious colonnaded courtyard with a narrow surrounding portico, here we find a rather smaller quadrangle with a very wide portico, far superior to those in the mosques of the Syrian Umayyads. In addition, the *mihrab* (*ill.* 3) or niche directed towards Mecca (a kind of Moslem high altar) is abnormally long. The Mosque of Abd al-Rahman I had eleven naves running from north to south, and because the walls of the Christian basilica were used the *mihrab* was set facing south and not on the azimuth of Mecca. In the years that followed the building underwent several alterations and extensions. Under Abd al-Rahman II the wall at the southern end was built in order to lengthen the naves; this involved the transfer of the *mihrab* to the end of the new wall. The present façade was erected in the reign of Abd al-Rahman III along the north side, with pillars and horse-shoe arches. This façade had become necessary to strengthen the northern end, designed only for the old structure, which threatened to collapse because the earlier alterations had lengthened the naves excessively and these were open to the courtyard at this point. At all events, the major renovation and extension of the Mosque took place during the reign of al-Haquem II. At that time the capital of the Caliphate had reached the highest point of its development and the number of the faithful who assembled for prayer in the Mosque on Fridays had reached such proportions that its walls were unable to contain them. This decided the Caliph to make extensions: the south wall was once more demolished and the eleven naves were lengthened, this time following the direction along which they already ran. In the final enlargement undertaken by al-Mansur, the builders were forced to change direction, since the structure had reached the banks of the Guadalquivir; they pulled down the eastern side and built eight more naves.

The Mosque was supported on pillars taken from ancient and Visigothic monuments. Because of the large space to be roofed, the installation of a series of simple arches would have resulted in a building that was too low and too unstable. The problem was solved by the construction of a double row of super-imposed arcades, the inspiration for which had probably come from the Roman aqueducts; Roman influence can also be seen in the formation of the arcades with their stones in an alternating brick and stone pattern (*ill.* 7). The arches are supported on thin columns. This method of construction gives a rising effect to the Spanish Arabic architecture of the Umayyads and their buildings seem to fan out upwards in contrast to Classical buildings which are notable for their rather solid appearance, caused by their slightly pyramidal shape. For his alterations, Abd al-Rahman II used the same type of arch, but the design of the capitals is influenced by Syrian and local traditions; there was

9. Part of the Moorish city wall at Cordoba; many parts are still standing.

10. The Patio de los Naranjos, the peaceful forecourt to the Cordoban Mosque.

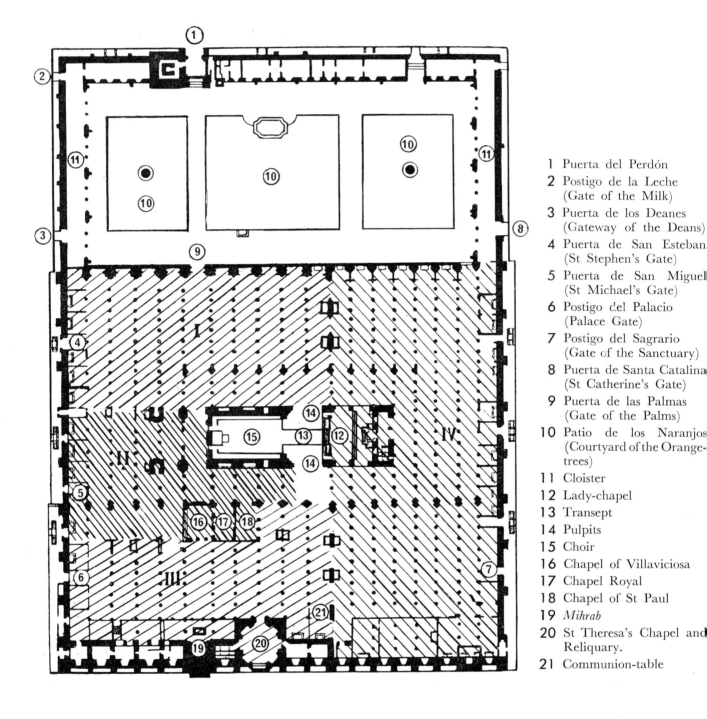

PLAN OF THE MOSQUE AT CORDOBA

1 Puerta del Perdón
2 Postigo de la Leche
(Gate of the Milk)
3 Puerta de los Deanes
(Gateway of the Deans)
4 Puerta de San Esteban
(St Stephen's Gate)
5 Puerta de San Miguel
(St Michael's Gate)
6 Postigo del Palacio
(Palace Gate)
7 Postigo del Sagrario
(Gate of the Sanctuary)
8 Puerta de Santa Catalina
(St Catherine's Gate)
9 Puerta de las Palmas
(Gate of the Palms)
10 Patio de los Naranjos
(Courtyard of the Orange-
trees)
11 Cloister
12 Lady-chapel
13 Transept
14 Pulpits
15 Choir
16 Chapel of Villaviciosa
17 Chapel Royal
18 Chapel of St Paul
19 *Mihrab*
20 St Theresa's Chapel and
Reliquary.
21 Communion-table

Area marked ' I ': naves built by Abd al-Rahman I; area marked ' II ': additions
by Abd al-Rahman II; area marked ' III ': additions by al-Haquem II; area
marked ' IV ': naves built by al-Mansur.

9

10

still no trace of any influence from the Abbasid Empire. Under al-Haquem II a cupola was inserted in the central nave and three other domes were placed in front of the *mihrab*. Until then the decoration had been austere, but now it was to become sumptuous. In the naves additional arches were super-imposed in the same way as before, but under the cupolas a new element appeared—foiled arches derived from the Eastern Abbasid Empire, intertwined in the vaulting to produce geometric figures. The cupolas, too, are of Eastern, mainly Persian, origin. A network of interlaced ribs supports each dome, possibly in imitation of the Persian bricked vaults. The keystones of the arches of the four cupolas are alternately plain and decorated. Floral motifs also appear, but here they have reached the ultimate in stylization, which was to become a characteristic of Andalusian Moslem art. Byzantium, too, had a hand in the decoration: al-Haquem asked the Emperor of Constantinople for mosaicists to adorn the extensions he had made; their work can still be seen on the *mihrab* and its cupola, on the door leading to the palace and on the Imam's Gate. Mesopotamian influences can be detected in the wooden roofs. Later, when al-Mansur had to extend this jewel of the Umayyad Empire, the largest mosque in all Islam at that time, he did not wish to depart from the style in which it was built and confined his work to enlarging it.

The main entrance to the Mosque, the Puerta del Perdón, is flanked by long turreted walls and fine pedimented porticos. It stands beneath what was once the minaret and is now the cathedral tower. This doorway leads to the *sahn* or Patio de los Naranjos (*ill.* 10), which has no adornment but the orange-trees that give it its name, some magnificent palm-trees and several fountains. As the Cordoban writer Ricardo Molina describes it, " it is a garden of water and sunshine, stone and shadow. Its austerity accords exactly with the simplicity of the art of the Caliphate, as well as with the noble Romano-Cordoban tradition and the very character of the people."

Molina goes on to say that the arches and pillars of the galleries at the eastern and western ends form a harmonious frame for the courtyard. These galleries date from the fifteenth century but are probably of Moslem origin, and contain the remains of the fine original panelling. If we enter the cathedral from this courtyard through the Puerta de las Palmas, also known as the Puerta de las Bendiciones, we shall see stretching before us the eleven naves built by Abd al-Rahman I from 785 onwards. Inside it is like an intricate, gloomy forest, in contrast with the shining Patio de los Naranjos. The innumerable shafts of the columns, made of jasper, marble and fine stone of every hue, intermingle before our gaze, all of them crowned by fantastically shaped capitals, some Roman, some Gothic, the rest Moorish. Unity is imposed by the red and white stripes of the arches, broken only by the *mihrab* and the tracery of the Villaviciosa Chapel. A pale, ghostly light pervades the magical air of the Mosque, inducing meditation or silent aesthetic contemplation. The elegant balance brought about by the long series of arcades surpasses every other feature. The horse-shoe arches resting on slender pillars, the semicircular arches rising above them and the interplay of the soaring columns combine to produce a magnificent structural effect. The additions of Abd al-Rahman II, al-Haquem II and al-Mansur heighten the brilliance of the setting where the foiled arch, of Mesopotamian origin, can be seen to advantage in the *mihrab* constructed by al-Haquem II. A most important decorative and architectural feature is the typically Cordoban technique of covering a quadrangular area

11. Flowers and white walls in a quiet corner of the ancient Judería or Ghetto of Cordoba.

45

Ivory casket, detail.

with spectacular, multi-coloured vaulting, similar to the opulent Byzantine mosaics to be seen on the wall of the *mihrab* or in the Chapel of Villaviciosa. This technique marked a clear aesthetic advance in the art of the Caliphate and undoubtedly influenced Western architecture in that period.

The Christian Cathedral was constructed within the Mosque. It stands in the midst of the Moorish pillars and the first sign of it cannot fail to produce a shock. Its contrast with the Arabic structure heightens not only the aesthetic differences between the two religions but also the clash of the architectural concepts of the two peoples. The Holy Roman Emperor Charles V, who ordered its construction, later expressed his regret for this artistic outrage.

The End of the Caliphate

Under Abd al-Rahman III the unity of al-Andalus was precarious and artificial. The Spain of the Caliphate, which consisted of a hybrid population of discordant Arabs and Berbers, Christians, Jews and Moslems, must have been difficult to subdue, let alone govern. The monarch understood perfectly that his authority was in the balance and that his person was under constant threat from the plots and revolts at Court; he therefore decided to live on the outskirts of his capital, protected by a foreign bodyguard and administration. These foreigners, wrongly called " Slavs ", in time developed into what can only be described as a caste. In this reign it is calculated that there were almost 14,000 of them. They took on the role of eunuchs and ran the harem and the palace; they acted as scribes and clerks and controlled the public administration; they served as soldiers and organized the army. These so-called " Slavs ", who were hated by Arabs, Berbers and Spaniards alike, came from the whole of the Mediterranean region. They were bought by the Jews in Black Sea and Levant ports, then sold in Spain, where they underwent special training. They were Galician Poles, Franks, Germans and Lombards. Some towns in the South of France apparently even produced eunuchs to swell the ranks of the " Slavs ". Verdun, it is said, was famous for this industry. This army of servants, palace officials and military officers was the Caliph's best instrument of government. He ruled by a military dictatorship, which relied on these foreigners for its very existence; thus the unifying factor in his empire came from outside. Even he was a foreigner; though his line had governed Spain for centuries, he was still only camping there, as Arabs and Turks always did in the lands through which they passed.

Abd al-Rahman III did not succeed in uniting the various peoples of his empire. Al-Mansur, the other outstanding ruler during the Caliphate, was also unsuccessful: he was a usurper who tried in vain to found a new dynasty to replace that of the Umayyads. This intruder, though he did not assume the title of Caliph, was the real ruler of the country in the time of the weak Hisham II, and was a dictator in the full sense of the term. From his youth, he had always had fantastic ambitions and the determination to seize power by any means that were to hand. The following anecdote about him has survived: one day, during the first years of the reign of al-Haquem II, son of Abd al-Rahman, al-Mansur was dining in a Cordoban garden with four fellow students. It was a gay party; only the future dictator was silent and sunk in deep thought. Finally he came out of his daydream and suddenly shouted:

Ivory casket, detail.

"There's no doubt about it! I shall rule this country one day..." His friends burst into laughter. But he added, without a change of expression, "each of you must tell me which post you would like in my government."

"All right," said one of the students, "these doughnuts are first class. If it's all the same to you, appoint me market inspector and I'll see that I always get plenty of them cheaply!"

Another of the company joined in: "I've always had a passion for these figs from my home town of Málaga. Make me *cadi* of that province."

"Since I love these gardens," said the third, "give me the post of Governor of Cordoba."

The fourth remained silent, annoyed by his companions' ambitious aspirations.

"You there, tell me what you want!" al-Mansur chided him. The other got up and pulled al-Mansur's beard, saying, "When you rule in Spain, you mad boaster, have my body covered in honey for all the flies to bite me, and make me ride through Cordoba on a donkey!"

Al-Mansur glared at him, but, in an effort to control his rage, replied, "Very well. You shall all have what you want. One day I shall remember what you have said."

It is said that he kept his word.

The real name of this young man with such a thirst for power was Abi Amir Mohammed. The Amirid Dynasty he tried to establish could rival the Umayyads in nobility. Al-Mansur ("the Victor")—the name he adopted much later—boasted of his descent from an ancient Yemeni family that included one of the few Arab chieftains who accompanied Tarik in the Conquest of Spain. In spite of his illustrious origin, he had modest beginnings. At first a scribe in the service of the *cadi* of Cordoba, he managed to obtain the post of treasurer in the service of young Abd al-Rahman, son of the Caliph al-Haquem III. This was the start of his rise to power. He lost no time in endearing himself to the Sultana Aurora, who was a Christian of Basque origin and who completely dominated the Caliph. He soon became her lover and thanks to this association he was appointed inspector of coinage, attorney of abeyant estates, Cadi of Seville and Niebla, and lastly chief of the *Chorta*, the militia formed to maintain internal order. When al-Haquem died al-Mansur managed, with the Grand Vizier's help, to bring about the assassination of a claimant to the throne who was supported by the powerful court eunuchs, that is to say, by the "Slav" party. From that moment, al-Mansur's career became a long sequence of acts of treachery and murder to eliminate, one by one, all his rivals. The Caliph, imprisoned by him in the old palace in Cordoba, allowed him to rule in his place. He had a palace built for himself on the edge of the capital, because he found Abd al-Rahman's Medina Azzahra inconveniently distant, and he considered it too dangerous to live in Cordoba itself. From his new palace, continually fighting his rivals, he governed an empire that stretched even further than that of Abd al-Rahman the Great. In the south, he secured the Caliphate's hold over the coastal region of Barbary, and in the north, he extended his rule as far as the Cantabrian Sea, capturing León and Santiago de Compostela. Never had Christendom faced such a critical situation: but, as always, such conquests were transitory.

The tyrant left Cordoba on the third of July, 977 and, by way of Coria and Vizeo, invaded Galicia. He was supported by a fleet that scoured the Atlantic coast, and in Vizeo his army was strengthened by some Christian counts who were his vassals. The campaign appears to have been particularly arduous because of the problem of forcing a way through that mountainous region, full of

12. Decoration and Hebrew inscription on the wall of the fourteenth-century synagogue in Cordoba.

48

streams, torrents and estuaries. The Christians used their normal tactic of flee-
ing before the attacker in order to draw him into the gorges and wild stretches
of country. At last, after setting fire to the venerable sanctuary of Padrón,
al-Mansur and his troops reached the gates of " the proud city of St James "
(Santiago). Its inhabitants had fled, as had those of Pamplona earlier
when that city was attacked by Abd al-Rahman. The Saracen army stole
everything that could be stolen and the city was laid waste, including the
Basilica of which " no trace remained ". However, al-Mansur, being a good
Moslem and therefore respecting a disciple of Christ, placed guards around the
tomb of St James, which was thus preserved. It seems that an ancient monk
was discovered sitting near the tomb. He was the only citizen who had not tried
to desert the relics of the Patron Saint of Spain. The tyrant asked him what
he was doing there. " Worshipping St James! " the old man replied simply.
Al-Mansur ordered that he should be spared his life and allowed to pray in peace.

When the victor returned to Cordoba the Moslems were greeted with the
sight of a host of Christian captives carrying the bells of Santiago and the doors
of the Cathedral on their shoulders through the streets. These finely wrought
doors were placed in the Mosque, and the bells seem to have been turned into
lampholders. The display of these trophies and the large number of Christian
prisoners, who were put to work on the extensions being made to the Mosque,
convinced the Moslems that the final rout of the enemies of Islam had taken
place. But the situation soon changed. Beset as he was by rivals inside his kingdom and by the counter-attack of the Christian armies outside, al-Mansur's
star soon set and with it all the might of the Caliphate. It must be recorded,
however, that he was a cultured ruler, as well as being a fanatic and a mystic.
He made a copy, in his own hand, of the text of the Koran, which he always
carried with him and constantly mused over. He would order all heretical
books that he came across to be destroyed. Taking the literal interpretation
of one of the *suras* of the Koran, he used to have the dust from his clothes and sandals collected during his campaigns against the Christians, because this dust,
according to the Koran, is pleasing to God. As a penance, he travelled dressed
in his shroud and constantly begged God for the favour of dying while fighting
the infidels; this favour was finally granted to him. When returning from his
last raid in Christian territory, after having burnt down the Monastery of San
Millán de la Cogolla, he died in a pious manner in Medinaceli.

At the height of the Caliphate, the Arab historians claim that Cordoba had
about half a million inhabitants, three thousand mosques, a hundred and thirteen thousand houses and three hundred public baths, without taking into
account its many suburbs. Of the city proper, nothing survives, apart from
the Mosque and some ruins of no artistic interest. This appears to indicate
that the buildings were generally not solidly built and that the *medina*, like most
Moslem cities today, was not monumental and was, from the outside at least,
architecturally undistinguished. It probably consisted of a maze of narrow lanes
and an agglomeration of small houses, with few openings and with unadorned
whitewashed walls. Of course, the richer houses would have been larger with
extensive gardens; but, like the poor dwellings, they would have no exterior
features to attract the attention of the passer-by. They were all of the old
Roman and Mediterranean type, with interior courtyards and walled gardens.
A text of Ibn Bashkuwal gives an account of how Greek and Roman remains
could be seen in Cordoba: " statues of silver and gilded bronze, from which

13. One of the many narrow streets in Morisco style that lead to the Mosque at Cordoba.

water spilled into bowls and then into pools and finely wrought marble shells." Here we can see that the Moslems discovered in what remained of Roman Cordoba, in the midst of their own dwellings, many of the main motifs of their interior decoration.

Cordoba today preserves many of the essential features of the Roman and of the Moslem city. The houses are now more open to the street, but under their gleaming coat of whitewash they are basically the same light structures of baked brick and adobe; the same bare and shining surfaces on which the slightest decorative feature takes on an unexpected value; the same crossroads amid the low houses, overshadowed by the square church towers that were once minarets and before that Visigothic belfries; the same tiny squares where the fragile clusters of jasmine fill the air with a thick, aphrodisiac fragrance, almost unbearably sweet; the same window-sills spilling flowers over the blinding whiteness of the walls, under a scorching sun.

As for the Mosque, although the Christians made many alterations, some of them disastrous, as their instigator, Charles V, admitted when he saw them, it still possesses enormous architectural interest and indescribable charm. No religious thoughts are evoked by those interminable rows of many-hued pillars and arches with their blood-coloured keystones; rather they conjure up a vision of lines of pergolas hung with flowers. Apart from the aesthetic effect, the emotional impact is rather different: in that forest of variegated marble one senses still the flitting shadows of the Mohammedans, swathed in their white cloaks, stealing barefoot over the cool slabs of the temple. One feels the presence of the Cordoba of the Caliphate here, more than anywhere else in the city.

Life in the Cordoban Caliph's court had developed a protocol that, during Abd al-Rahman III's reign, became more and more strict; this was especially apparent in the great palace receptions and ceremonies, when the Caliph appeared surrounded by a splendid entourage. There, everyone had his exact place according to his position in the palace or the government. Only among his closest intimates would the Caliph permit himself a certain familiarity. These small gatherings occurred frequently and were enlivened by music and dancing supplied by artists of both sexes, by the verses of hired poets and by the antics of fools and clowns. Most of the duties of the Caliph's household were the responsibility of the "Slav" eunuchs who had access to the royal harem. The whole court presented a motley picture of the comings and goings of richly dressed people, amid a scene of opulence that did not quite blend with the half-hidden background of violence. The long century of the Caliphate exemplified a particular society and culture. This society consisted of Orientals and Spaniards, free men and slaves, professional soldiers and merchants, Jewish teachers, embassies from the Christian kingdoms and a host of other assorted people. The harem girls were sold by the merchants who had brought them from the Baltic. In the time of Abd al-Rahman III alone, there were 6,300 such women in the palace, purchased for domestic service and royal lovemaking. Important ceremonies, the swearing of oaths by heirs, and the reception of embassies took place in the rooms of the royal Alcázar which stood on the banks of the Guadalquivir.

At the same time, the Eastern way of life set its mark, from the outset, on the Spanish population, who took to wearing brightly coloured clothes, caps and turbans, burnouses, clogs and rope-soled sandals — these last are still the usual footwear in the South of Spain. This important market was supplied by flourishing industries: silk from Almería, Seville and Granada; leather from Saragossa;

14. Twelfth-century Moorish silk tapestry.

52

and tooled leather from Cordoba. These industries not only supplied Moslem Spain but also exported their products to the northern Christian territories where the princes and nobles had clothes of Moorish cloth, and weapons and leather goods which had originated in Moorish territory but which were fashioned in the North. There also circulated in the Christian areas coins of the Caliphate minted at the *Ceca* or royal mint in Cordoba, such as gold *dinars* and silver *dirhems*.

This brilliant Moslem society lived in towns and in the country, where they built wonderful villas, farms and *almunias* (country houses). The structure of the Andalusian Moorish house was very similar to that of the Roman, but had the *alcoba* or bedroom at the rear. There also abounded at Court and in the Caliphate cities lyric poets who wrote *zéjeles* in praise of wine and the refined life; thinkers who were adapting the Aristotelian philosophy to their particular outlook; and physicians, scientists and mathematicians, who bequeathed to Europe an excellent compendium of knowledge, which they had obtained by combining Eastern experience with Western investigation.

It is interesting to record the life led by Moslem women during the Caliphate. Each woman remained from childhood in the harem, in her mother's care, and only rarely, if she lived in a large city, would she attend school, in any case only before she was nubile. On reaching womanhood she began her life of mysterious seclusion. Her father or her guardians would arrange her marriage, without her having ever met her husband beforehand. The marriage was purely a civil contract and, although in theory she had some rights, the Moslem wife had to share the affection and wealth of her husband with the other wives that the law permitted him. Divorce worked in favour of the husband. If he was sufficiently wealthy, he could have, in addition, as many slave-girls as he wished. They were the instruments of pleasure of their masters, who were generally caliphs or magnates, and enlivened their orgies and feastings. Some of them managed through their infatuated lords to control the purse-strings and even to bring their influence to bear on politics. Occasionally, Moslem women were impelled by love or desire to flout the rigidity of the law and have secret love-affairs arranged by the bawds of the city. Poets sang of their mistresses or of the princes' favourites and from them we learn that the Spanish Moslems had a high regard for generously proportioned women. The fair-haired girls from Galicia or the Basque Country were in great demand; because of this some astute traders used tricks and disguises to pass off Andalusian women as Christians from the North.

The Cordoban people of the Caliphate had a great love of books. In the western suburb alone about 170 women earned their living by copying manuscripts. Every year about 60,000 books were produced in Cordoba. The Caliph al-Haquem built up a library of 400,000 volumes, and the nobles followed his example. There was a flourishing book market where rare or *de luxe* books were auctioned. When al-Mansur came to power, he wanted to ingratiate himself with the *alfaquíes* or Moslem theologians and ordered an expurgation of the Caliph's library, greatly reducing its holding. Many bibliographical treasures were lost, too, during internal revolts and, of course, at the time of the Christian Reconquest.

This world of opulence and pageantry, culture and refinement, which witnessed wild orgies and the last of the military raids, bore within it the seeds of the imminent decline of the Caliphate and its might. A new epoch was soon to open, in which two cities in particular were to flourish in Moslem al-Andalus: Seville and, above all, Granada, shortly to blaze with all the exquisite and decadent brilliance of an empire nearing its close.

15. One of the outer doors of the Cordoban Mosque. The restrained decoration and the horse-shoe arch are characteristic of the architecture of the early Caliphs.

16. (*p.* 57) Remains of a lattice, blind arches and tiny columns in the western outer wall of the Cordoban Mosque.

17. (*p.* 58) One of the cupolas in the quadrangular chapels of the eastern part of the Mosque at Cordoba. The decoration between the ribs may be of Persian origin.

Genealogical Table of the Umayyad Caliphs of Cordoba

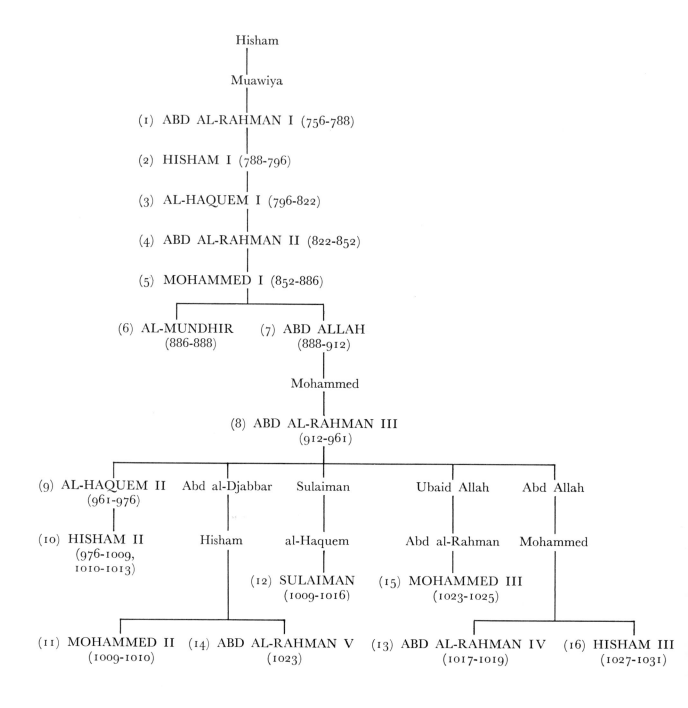

Hisham

Muawiya

(1) ABD AL-RAHMAN I (756-788)

(2) HISHAM I (788-796)

(3) AL-HAQUEM I (796-822)

(4) ABD AL-RAHMAN II (822-852)

(5) MOHAMMED I (852-886)

(6) AL-MUNDHIR (886-888)   (7) ABD ALLAH (888-912)

Mohammed

(8) ABD AL-RAHMAN III (912-961)

(9) AL-HAQUEM II (961-976)   Abd al-Djabbar   Sulaiman   Ubaid Allah   Abd Allah

(10) HISHAM II (976-1009, 1010-1013)   Hisham   al-Haquem   Abd al-Rahman   Mohammed

(12) SULAIMAN (1009-1016)   (15) MOHAMMED III (1023-1025)

(11) MOHAMMED II (1009-1010)   (14) ABD AL-RAHMAN V (1023)   (13) ABD AL-RAHMAN IV (1017-1019)   (16) HISHAM III (1027-1031)

SEVILLE

La mar no tiene naranjas,
ni Sevilla tiene amor.

García Lorca

SEVILLE

AL-MANSUR'S DEATH was immediately followed by a series of revolts, and the Caliph's authority was put in jeopardy. Shortly afterwards, the Caliphate fell and the unity of the Empire was shattered. The central machinery of power crumbled into impotence, and anarchy and secessionism held sway throughout the territory of the Spanish Moslems. Ambitious adventurers began to seize power in many cities and areas of al-Andalus, creating new kingdoms that varied in size and strength. Among these new monarchs were many from the old Arab families long established in Spain; others sprang from the first Berbers to reach the Peninsula who by then were almost completely Hispanized; yet others were Berbers recently brought to Spain by al-Mansur. The latter included the Zirids, the first kings of Granada. In addition, the adventuring petty monarchs who set up their own thrones after the fall of the Caliphate included the " Slavs " of the Cordoban Court who established their domains in the eastern part of al-Andalus. Of this mass of tiny states, which were called *taifas*, only a few stood the test of time; among these more solid *taifas* figured Seville, Granada, Badajoz, Almería, Toledo and Saragossa, all of which managed greatly to enlarge their boundaries. All of them frequently fought and betrayed one another and exploited their own inhabitants; most of them turned their capital cities into centres of culture and pleasure.

This state of affairs, which followed the breaking up of the Empire, came about in the first years of the eleventh century when the viziers abolished the capital status of Cordoba. At once the provinces broke the ties uniting them with the former capital. The Arab monarchy withdrew from the scene and each chieftain created his own domain. The Berbers ruled in the South, the " Slavs " in the East, the pure-blooded Arabs in the South-West and the Christians in the North. Thus, because of the tribal outlook of the Arabs and North Africans, their domestic feuds and their quarrels, their unrestrained individualism, the unity of Spain was in greater danger than ever. There no longer existed a great Moslem monarchy to stand as an example for the Christian kingdoms of the North; the sight of Arab anarchy could only encourage their feudal anarchy.

This chaos continued for centuries despite the efforts of some of the Spanish sovereigns to re-establish a unity that had always been difficult to achieve. The situation was a great source of weakness for Spain; but, although the country lost power and political importance, it gained in the sphere of culture, if not in civilization. Between the death of al-Mansur and the invasions of the Almoravids and the Almohads, a period of nearly a century, the Arabs became noticeably

Hispanized, their religious fanaticism waned and they developed a taste for luxurious living with an intellectual tone. It was rather like the development that took place in Italy at the time of the *podestàs* and the small city states. These Moslem kinglets, softened by the luxury and mildness of their surroundings, slowly lost their warlike tendencies; their Arab and African soldiers changed in the same way. Because of this, they became more and more obliged to employ Christian mercenaries to defend their possessions for them. These mercenaries were such a permanent feature of the scene that many Castilians, Basques, Navarrese, Aragonese and Catalans earned their entire livelihood by the profession of arms.

The monarchs who engaged these soldiers, who formed a kind of *condottieri*, were generally dominated by their viziers or ministers, who were the real governors of the palace, always preoccupied by intrigues and ambitions, and usually succeeding in making themselves all-powerful; they often shared their masters' taste for pageantry and learning. Among these men was the famous Vizier of Almería, Abu 'l-Abbas, an avaricious petty tyrant who had, however, built himself a palace that was regally adorned. He had five hundred female singers in his harem, a library of thousands of richly bound volumes, was a great man of letters and an avid reader. He wrote very well and his epistles were considered masterpieces of their kind. Not all these petty kings were the pawns of their viziers; some were active, self-willed and even rather coarse-natured, well able to keep their ministers at bay and impose their own wishes. Of these, a few stand out; men of originality, well worth examining in detail in order to gain an impression of Moslem Spain at the time in all its many facets; the picture is appreciably different from that of the Cordoban Caliphate.

The two most important of these minor sovereigns held the thrones of the most significant kingdoms during the period of the *taifas*: Granada and Seville. These rival monarchs were Badis of Granada and al-Mutadid of Seville. The last dictator of al-Andalus, al-Mansur, although he was of Arab origin, had everywhere placed Berbers in command to maintain his usurped rule. His tyranny had alienated Arabs and Spaniards alike and they had long wished to rid themselves of the alien African barbarians and expel them to the far side of the Straits of Gibraltar. The opposing factions of Berbers and Arabs finally produced the two leaders they deserved: the Berber Badis and the Arab al-Mutadid.

Both were extraordinary men: Badis, brutal and bloodthirsty, epitomized the nomad African in his wild, uncivilized condition; although, he had been born in Spain, in the soft and beautiful surroundings of Granada, he was an uneducated Berber who spoke Arabic badly and prided himself on his ignorance and sullenness, as well as on his sensuality and unquenchable thirst for good Andalusian wine. His grandfather Zawi, who had always been homesick for Africa and who finally died there, had made Granada a capital city. Habbus, the second of the Dynasty of the Zirids or Banu Ziris and father of Badis, had fortified the new capital with encircling walls and constructed an *al-kasr* or royal palace, the magnificence of which was extolled in all the contemporary chronicles. Despite his power, he lived simply, without exercising great authority, leaving the business of government to Samuel Ibn Naghzala, a Jew, who had dazzled him with his astuteness, eloquence and knowledge of the Arabic language and its literature. Meanwhile, his son Badis, between bouts of drunkenness and debauchery, would lead out his men on predatory raids, cutting off heads with excessive frequency. He was brave to the point of insanity; he would be seized by sudden and frightening fits

18. Detail of the *attawriq* decoration on an arched doorway in the western part of the addition made to the Cordoban Mosque in the tenth century by al-Haquem II. The floral motifs show an increased sophistication.

of rage, and he often took on the role of hangman and executioner, carrying out the sentence without scruples of any kind.

Badis's rival, al-Mutadid, King of Seville, had a similar nature; they both possessed certain debauched and vicious habits, such as their cruelty, which in any case was common at the time. Contemptuous of the prohibitions of the Koran, al-Mutadid enjoyed wine as much as his enemy in Granada. For him, night was a time for feasting and vice, and he revelled with his favourites and courtiers until daybreak. His harem was one of the best stocked in Spain: it is stated that the number of its women approached eight hundred. This exaggerated sensuality ran parallel with a sinister sense of humour. Following the example of the last Caliphs of Cordoba, he had flowers planted in the craniums of his decapitated enemies and decorated his terraces with these macabre flowerpots, all labelled with the names of their former owners. A special fate was reserved for the heads of princes: they were kept in leather caskets, like jewels, and the little despot would take them out from time to time to gloat over them, much as misers are said to gloat over their gold.

Al-Mutadid ordered gallows to be erected in the courtyard of his palace and had them adorned with the heads of chieftains, thus providing gruesome replacements for the flowering trees more normally used to decorate such places. The historians of his time assure us that not one of his contemporaries could match him in energy, ruthlessness and violence. They compared him with al-Mansur. He instilled terror in every one of his subjects, particularly after he slew, in cold blood, his eldest son Ismail, who had been destined to succeed him. From some information that had reached his ears, al-Mutadid knew that, although his son treated him affably to his face, he secretly longed for his father's death. The king ignored this information until one night, when Ismail was drunk, he attempted with the aid of some slaves and mercenaries to scale the walls of his father's residence, with intent to get rid of him. The gate-keepers and the guards awoke, but all the attackers managed to escape, except one. Under torture, this slave confessed that the attack had been planned by Ismail. In view of this evidence, al-Mutadid ordered Ismail's arrest, confiscated his goods and cut off his head. " From then onwards he inspired a much greater respect among all the members of his household," wrote the historian al-Marrakushi.

The same chronicler gives an account of how al-Mutadid rid himself of a blind man from the outskirts of Seville, who used to inveigh against him in public. The king deprived him of much of his substance, leaving him destitute. The blind man then went to Mecca and there cursed al-Mutadid publicly every day. When the latter got wind of this he summoned before him a man who was about to make a pilgrimage to the holy city. Al-Mutadid handed him a small box that contained some coins smeared with poison. " Do not open the box," he told the messenger. " Hand it to the blind man in Mecca and give him my compliments." The pilgrim reached Mecca, sought out the blind man and gave him the box, with al-Mutadid's message. The man could not believe it and said, " How is it possible that the man who ruined me in Seville now sends me gifts to Arabia? " At last the messenger managed to convince him and he accepted the box. He opened it at once, took out one of the coins and bit it to test its genuineness. The poison soon took effect and he died before the next morning.

It is astonishing that a man who lived in a distant corner of al-Andalus should have taken such pains to liquidate a harmless enemy on the other side of Islam. This was not al-Mutadid's only act of revenge, however. He also avenged himself

19. Marble capital excavated at the site of Medina Azzahra, near Cordoba.

on a muezzin who had fled to Toledo and there used to curse his former king every sunrise, thinking himself out of reach of his hatred. Al-Mutadid did not rest until he had the poor muezzin killed and his head brought to Seville.

Of the princes who ruled the lands around Seville, the fiercest and most important belonged to the Banu Birzal, a Berber tribe that had settled in Carmona and the surrounding areas. By using force at times and cunning at others, al-Mutadid managed to reduce their power and sow seeds of discontent among them, until finally he succeeded in banishing them, becoming the undisputed ruler of the region.

Let us consider one example of the cunning means by which he used to further his own interests. In Carmona he had a spy who kept him informed of the Berbers' affairs. One day, when the king wanted to send a message to this spy, he summoned to his presence a poor man who was simple and guileless. He ordered him to strip off his clothes, had him dressed in a tunic, in the folds of which lay the hidden message, and told him, " Go to Carmona. When you are near the town, cut some firewood and make it into a bundle. Then go on into the town and look for the place frequented by the firewood sellers. But sell your bundle only to the man who offers you five *dirhems*." All the details had been arranged beforehand by al-Mutadid and his agent in Carmona. Outside the city, the poor man picked firewood, making up a very small faggot, for that was the first time he had done such work. He went into the town and sat down in the firewood market. Some purchasers approached him but went off in fits of laughter when he asked five *dirhems* for such a small bundle. There he remained all day, continually teased by the buyers. Finally, al-Mutadid's agent appeared and asked him the price of his faggot. When the man answered " Five *dirhems*, " the agent said, " Very well. I shall buy it. Carry it to my house." Seller and buyer made off to the spy's house, where the fellow put down his burden and was paid. As he made for the door, the spy said, " Where are you going at this time of night? The streets are not safe. Spend the night here and tomorrow morning you may leave."

The fellow was taken to a room where his host served him with food and asked him, " Where do you come from? " " From the outskirts of Seville, " was the reply.

" Why did you come here, my friend, knowing the cruelty of the Berbers and their bloodthirstiness? "

" In order to earn my living, " answered the poor man, without revealing that al-Mutadid had sent him.

His host then said, " Go to bed and take off your clothes to sleep more comfortably."

The fellow did as he was told and went off to sleep. The spy then took his tunic, unstitched its folds and removed the letter. He then inserted his reply and sewed up the garment again so that there was no sign that it had been disturbed. The next day, the simple man dressed and set off for Seville. There he presented himself at the royal palace and was received by al-Mutadid. The king ordered him to take off his tunic and gave him a set of fine clothes. The poor man went off happily, unaware of the reason for his journey to Carmona.

This story, told by Marrakushi, is rather ingenuous, yet it illustrates the lengths of cunning to which the King of Seville was prepared to go in order to achieve his political aims.

On the other hand, al-Mutadid was fond of learning and tried his hand at

20. One of the numerous fountain basins that once adorned the Palace of Medina Azzahra. This example is in marble and the ornamentation is restrained.

21. Fragment of alabaster relief excavated at Medina Azzahra, showing the interlaced foliage motifs characteristic of Moorish decoration.

20

21

poetry like almost all great Arabs, as well as employing a veritable regiment of poets. Unlike his rival in Granada, he took pride in speaking Arabic elegantly and boasted of his erudite accomplishments. He was a diplomat and an armchair strategist who never led out his troops in person. Calculating, astute and subtly treacherous, he did not shrink from any device advantageous to his kingdom or his personal grandeur: he was a forerunner of Machiavelli, an early Borgia.

His son, al-Mutamid, was a very different type of person. This young prince, who followed his father on the throne of Seville, was a classic example of a Hispanized Arab, and his intellect was more developed than that of his father. The first information the chroniclers give us of young al-Mutamid is of his involvement in a passionate friendship and a great love affair which surround him with an aura of romantic poetry. When he was only twelve years old, his father appointed him Governor of Silves, capital of the Algarve. This region is one of the most picturesque in Portugal, and Silves itself, in the eyes of Moslems of the period was a place of delight and enchantment. During his stay there, the young prince came completely under the influence of a local poet, Ibn Ammar, who was rather older than he, a quite unscrupulous adventurer, somewhat gauche and coarse in appearance, but extremely shrewd and intelligent. Ibn Ammar, though of humble birth, had a wide cultural background. He had first studied in his birthplace, Silves, and later in Cordoba. Since he had real talent as a poet, he set off on his travels through Spain, selling his verses to the highest bidder. At that time poets were paid to be panegyrists and polemicists and more or less undertook the role of the present-day public relations man. But Ibn Ammar's sorry appearance and poor condition did him considerable harm and he did not manage to achieve the success for which he had hoped among the nobility. Weary of his wandering life of misery and hunger, he returned to Silves in the hope that his fellow countrymen would be readier to recognize his poetic talent. He arrived there in a forlorn state, possessing only the mule which he rode, but which he could not afford to feed. At this difficult juncture, he remembered a rich merchant of the city who might extricate him from his predicament. He addressed to him a eulogistic poem in which, while flattering the merchant's vanity, he told of his own penury and his mount's hunger. The merchant, who must have had some sense of humour, replied by sending him merely a bag of oats.

It was then that Ibn Ammar became acquainted with young al-Mutamid and from that moment poetry played an important part in their relationship. Al-Mutamid had far greater literary pretensions than his father and the verses of the Silves tramp poet thrilled him so much that he made him his Vizier and favourite. It was a tyrannical friendship: al-Mutamid could not live without his new friend; and such excessive favour disturbed Ibn Ammar, perhaps because he knew of the risk involved in putting his trust in princes. One night while sleeping, the poet dreamt he heard a voice saying: " You poor wretch! Al-Mutamid will be your murderer! " This prophetic dream frightened him so much that he tried to flee from the palace. But he was stopped by the guards. The next morning, the two friends gave each other explanations of the night's events and al-Mutamid spoke so affectionately to his favourite and so demonstrated his friendship for him that he soon forgot his bad dream. So the life of friendship and pleasure continued with greater intensity than before. When al-Mutamid went to Seville, Ibn Ammar went with him and acted as confidant in his love-affairs. There, one day, during a popular fiesta on the banks of the Guadalquivir, held in the walk called the Prado de Plata (Meadow of Silver), the two friends

22. Arches in one of the main halls, possibly the throne-room, at present being restored at the Palace of Medina Azzahra.

mingled incognito with the crowd and amused themselves by improvising lines of verse. Al-Mutamid flung out a couplet for which Ibn Ammar, momentarily nonplussed, could find no answer, when a young woman who was standing nearby gave a quick reply. This woman was the famous al-Rumaikiya, who was soon to become al-Mutamid's mistress and later was to take her place at his side as his wife and queen.

Who was this al-Rumaikiya whom both Moslems and Christians surrounded with an aura of legend? She was probably a Christian as she was a slave and a muleteer, an unusual employment for a Moslem woman. This occupation has always been associated with poetry in Spain and this adventurous base-born girl possessed sufficient talent to excel among the wits of the Court. Moreover, she must certainly have had a great deal of charm, beauty, and a very intelligent coquetry, because young al-Mutamid fell madly in love with her. Prince Don Juan Manuel, in his curious book *El conde Lucanor*, tells of a delightful incident in al-Rumaikiya's life: once, gazing out of a window in Cordoba at al-Mutamid's side she saw something she had never seen before—the Cordoban Plain stretching white and shining before them under a fall of snow. The sight so thrilled her that she longed to see it again and begged her lover to let her have her wish without her having to journey to lands where snow was common. To satisfy his favourite's caprice, al-Mutamid had countless almond trees planted on the Cordoban Plain, and so, every year at the end of winter, he showed al-Rumaikiya the Andalusian countryside completely covered in a fragrant mantle of snowlike blossom. On another occasion, capricious al-Rumaikiya saw some barefooted women treading the red clay that was used for making bricks and had an immediate and uncontrollable desire to do the same. Al-Mutamid at once ordered the palace yard to be filled with aromatic spices mixed with rose water until the courtyard became a pool of perfume, which he then invited al-Rumaikiya and her slave-girls to tread.

In the meantime, despite the sinister prophecy, the friendship between Ibn Ammar and al-Mutamid continued. But soon the prince's father, distrusting their close relationship, banished his son's confidant. The poet had to take refuge in the Moslem Court of Saragossa until the old king died, when al-Mutamid sent for his friend and appointed him Governor of the Algarve, the post he himself had occupied previously. But Ibn Ammar did not rule there long, for al-Mutamid could not get on without him, and he was recalled and made first minister. There is no doubt that it was at his instigation that al-Mutamid embarked on a campaign against Cordoba, which he captured after several reverses; he immediately ordered the crucifixion of the chieftain who had defended the city.

Life in the Alcázar of Seville must have had its problems: al-Mutamid's enemies were constantly on the watch and serious affairs of state frequently cut short more pleasant occupations. Ibn Ammar urged another expedition, this time against Murcia. The kingdom was occupied and Ibn Ammar made governor of the newly won region. Then began the favourite's fall from grace. Filled with greed, he made himself master of Murcia and kept himself too aloof from his sovereign. Ibn Ammar had mortal enemies among the advisers surrounding al-Mutamid, and these persuaded the king that his old friend now had treacherous designs. Fearing the enraged king's vengeance, Ibn Ammar fled once more to Saragossa. The former friends then began hitting out at each other with epigrams and satirical poems, but this bloodless battle had a tragic outcome. Ibn Ammar was captured in an ambush and brought before al-Mutamid. After spend-

23. Stylized bronze stag, celebrated not only for its intrinsic beauty, but because it is one of the rare examples of animal sculpture in Spanish Moslem art. Height without base $19^3/_4''$.

24. Finely wrought casket in ivory, dating from the time of the Cordoban Caliphate. The very rare representation of men and animals suggests that it may be the work of a Mozarab craftsman.

25. Stylized floral decoration on an ivory coffer made in the Cordoban workshops during the Caliphate.

26. Detail of the delicate ivory-work on a casket fashioned in Cordoba.

23   24

25

26

ing some time in the dungeons of Seville, the poet once more managed to win back the friendship of his king. This reconciliation was, however, short-lived: one day al-Mutamid became enraged by Ibn Ammar's boasting and chased him through the rooms of the palace. The favourite fell to his knees and begged for mercy but the king's anger was not so easily assuaged; he brandished an axe and brought it down on Ibn Ammar's head, leaving him dead amid a sea of blood. After so many twists of fortune, the prophecy had been fulfilled.

These stories shed considerable light on the disposition and behaviour of the minor kings of the *taifas*. Not even the soft and pampered life of their courts could extinguish the barbarous habits their ancestors had brought from Africa. They were sophisticated and given to affectation; but their sophistication did not entirely blot out the undertone of cruelty that occasionally manifested itself. They also possessed traits of a different calibre, which counterbalanced their more evil instincts. They were, it is true, more sensual than their predecessors, but they were also more cultured and more learned. As their abilities in warfare declined, they became clever diplomats and effective politicians. Religious intolerance had disappeared: they were not yet complete sceptics, but they practised a religion that was more humane and less rigorous. The lands of Andalusia must possess some quality which causes the warlike spirit of all its invaders to fade. Phoenicians, Goths, Romans and Moslems all found in those quiet and fruitful places their respective Capuas.

Before Castile began gradually to reconquer the whole of al-Andalus, two new waves of invasion were to reach the Peninsula from North Africa. The first was that of the Almoravid tribes of the Sahara only recently converted to Islam, who landed in Spain towards the middle of the eleventh century and occupied a large portion of the country. They came at the request of the *taifa* kings, who enlisted their aid against the military advances of the Christian King Alfonso VI. The Almoravids occupied the whole of al-Andalus and unified it once more. But this unity was not to last long; another invading wave, this time from the Atlas Mountains, was to put an end to the power of the Almoravids. These were the Almohads, fierce warriors and fanatic Mohammedans, who did not suffer a single setback until they were utterly and finally defeated by a coalition of several Christian kingdoms at the great Battle of Las Navas de Tolosa in 1212.

One of the results of this double invasion was a new Africanization of the South of Spain. Christians, Jews and Spanish Moslems were subdued and decimated. But this state of affairs was soon to change: both the Almoravids and the Almohads were eventually caught up and absorbed by the civilization they had conquered. Once more the mysterious power of the natural surroundings and culture of Andalusia had made itself felt: Seville and Granada had conquered again; and Granada became the centre of what remained of al-Andalus under the rule of the last Moorish royal line, the Nasrid Dynasty.

* * *

The artistic and cultural development of the Spanish Moslems follows almost an opposite course to that of their political and military history: when royal power was at its peak, artistic creation was at its lowest point; but at a time of political decadence there was aesthetic greatness. The artistic skills of the

27. Twelfth-century door-knocker on the Puerta del Perdón at Seville Cathedral.

28. The Torre del Oro, built by the Almohads at the beginning of the thirteenth century, which guards the entrance to the port of Seville on the River Guadalquivir. The tower was originally decorated with gilded tiles.

Dancing Gipsy, by Gustave Doré.

Spanish Moors are particularly well expressed in their architecture, not to mention their fine lyric poetry, from which sprang many literary developments in Southern Europe. On the other hand, sculpture and painting, as we understand them, were virtually unknown and if they were practised it was merely in the form of abstract decoration.

There is a common belief in the West that the Moslem religion utterly prohibits any artistic representation of a living creature. All that is certain is that any kind of religious image is forbidden. Otherwise, there is not a single line of the Koran that supports the belief, not even in its detailed instructions. Nevertheless, the Hadiths, a collection of sayings, acts and expressions of the Prophet, various compilations of which go back to the eleventh century, clearly demonstrate a hostile attitude to painting and sculpture. This work declares that makers of images that represent living beings are " the worst members of mankind ". The possession of such images is as grave an offence as having a dog in the house: both the image and the dog—a vile and despised animal—will prevent the " angel of pardon " from entering the house, a state of affairs almost as serious as that brought about by tattooing oneself or charging interest on loans. The prohibition is less trenchant when these images occur in parts of the house which the Hadiths regard as degraded: they are allowed without question on carpets and cushions, since to tread, sit or lie on an object immediately debases it. Other subjects could be represented with less risk: trees and other things in which " no breath of life resides ". Several historical factors are responsible for this prohibitive attitude, the most important being Semitic influence, for it was written in the Book of Exodus: " Thou shalt not make unto thee any graven image, or any likeness of any thing that is in heaven above, or that is in the earth beneath, or that is in the water under the earth."

Nevertheless, Spain is the only Western country in the Islamic world where we find a trace of mural pictorial decoration at the end of the Middle Ages. This mural can be found on the wall of a portico in the place now known as the Torre de las Damas of the Alhambra Palace in Granada and is attributed to the first half of the fourteenth century. The extremely small size of the human figures represented in the painting, which are placed on an overlapping strip (each horseman is scarcely eight inches high), may indicate a possible connection with the art of the miniature. Despite some deterioration, the subjects are easily discernible, as are the colours of the gold and more than a dozen other shades used. The painting includes some figures on horse-back, domestic scenes of groups of Moors, both male and female, apparently gathered for a celebration, huntsmen spurring their mounts, a lion and a monster, riders returning to their camp bringing women, slaves in chains, camels, pack-mules and sheep. Although the subjects are varied, there is little movement in the painting and no attempt to fill the whole space; the scenes and figures follow one another without logical connection, against a bare background. There is a clear sign of the presence of certain elements from almost contemporary Persian painting and of connections with the older art of decoration from Syrian enamelled vases, as well as of a general association with the miniatures of Christian Spain. These East-West connections have great importance in that they demonstrate how Islam, despite local variations, shared the same interests throughout its territory and possessed a characteristic artistic expression from its beginnings to the end of the Middle Ages.

The Alhambra has other examples of the representation of living figures in

Moslem art: the lions in the famous Patio de los Leones and those in the Patio de la Alberca. Moreover, there are others at the washing trough in the Palace of Medina Azzahra in Cordoba. But these vestiges are so rare that they should hardly be taken into account. It is in the structure and decoration of religious, civic and functional buildings that Arabic culture is most clearly revealed. However, when one uses the expression " Arabic art " it is easy to make the mistake, as the critic Gaya Nuño has pointed out, " of concluding that the aesthetic forms developed by the conquering Moslems from the Caliph Ali onwards possessed a theme of their own, a particular architectural arrangement and, in short, a cultural nucleus from which the other arts sprang. For this was not the case; the only types of Arabic buildings that preserve a certain unity of structure are the mosque and the palace, though they always absorb the traditional legacies of the conquered Latin or Byzantine countries. Moslem Spain or al-Andalus was no exception to the general rule. When the Moslem invaders reached the Guadalquivir, they lacked any culture apart from the Koran, and it was only the marvellous theological discipline of the conquerors and their fresh organizing spirit that brought together scattered elements to form a national art—an art which we cannot find adjectives sufficiently adequate to extol."

From the first attempts at building by the Moors who arrived with Tarik and Musa to the last stone of Nasrid architecture at Granada, the architecture of the Spanish Moslems went through many different stages that intermingled and overlapped. Perhaps it reached its most grandiose moment, as far as size and solidity are concerned, during the Umayyad period. It was then that the world-famous Mosque at Cordoba and the Palace of Medina Azzahra were built. After the fall of the Umayyads and the disintegration of the Cordoban Caliphate, this architecture lost some of its impetus and grandeur but it gained in refinement and delicacy. Moorish art went through various new stages in the post-Umayyad period; the most significant are those of the Mozarabs, the *taifas*, the Almoravids, the Almohads, the Mudejars and the Nasrid Dynasty.

The art of the Mozarabs or Christians who lived in the Moslem communities scarcely seems to have any points of contact with the art of the Umayyads: the magnificence of the latter stands out in sharp contrast with the simplicity and virtual poverty of the former. Whereas the Moslems until then had shown themselves to be decorators rather than architects in the true sense, the Mozarabs followed traditional Christian designs. They used horse-shoe arches that were definitely of Visigothic origin. In less than a dozen of their churches are slight Oriental influences to be seen—a few, for instance, have examples of the Arabic ribbed dome.

Very little is known of the architecture of the *taifas*, in the first period of the ninth century. The only important building of this epoch was the Mosque of the Aljafería, built by the Emir Ibn Djafar in Saragossa. It is all that remains of the country mansion known as the Aljafería, which belonged to the rulers of that kingdom. It enjoyed great fame at the time and chronicles and literary texts always call it " the palace of gaiety ": its owners must have spent many delightful hours in it. One of them, al-Muktadir, wrote a small eulogy: " O palace of happiness! O hall of gold! You have fulfilled my desires. I would covet nothing else, though I had no other kingdom than these." The style of the building had evolved from the art of the Umayyads, especially from the sumptuous style of al-Haquem II. The decoration followed the pattern of the earlier style, but with a more varied development: the lines intertwine more and more and

78

have two new motifs, simple symmetrical and asymmetrical palms. The decoration of the Aljafería is, in short, poorer than that of the Caliphate, but attains a minutely elaborate quality that might be called baroque.

The art of the Almoravids did not develop on Andalusian soil. Rather it consisted of Andalusian art evolving in another land, since the Almoravid Sultan Ali ben Yusuf sent for Peninsular craftsmen to go to Africa. This art was characterized by the harmony it struck between the sense of order of the art of the Caliphate and the richness of that of the *taifas*. The rich, complex adornments are subjected to a strict order, with a harmonic line that blots out the sense of disordered and excessive voluptuousness of the earlier style.

The religious puritanism of the Almohads, and their recently acquired faith, is reflected in their architecture. Their buildings are more extensive and monumental than those of the earlier periods, mainly because they used better materials and considered structure more important than decoration. Theirs is an art that is restrained and austere, and lacks the luxurious air of most Spanish Moslem building. Indeed, austerity is the main characteristic of Almohad art and the Giralda Tower of Seville is a good example of this, though perhaps it is more richly decorated than was customary in the architecture of the Almohads in North Africa.

* * *

After the fall of the Cordoban Caliphate, Seville became the most important city in Moorish Spain until its conquest by Ferdinand III. Seville's greatest period took place under Almoravid and Almohad rule. The Almohad Caliph Abu Yakub Yusuf was particularly involved in the embellishment and the enlarging of the city. The chroniclers of that period left excellent accounts of its brilliance; drawing on these for much of the detail, the historian Sánchez Albornoz offers us a vivid picture of Seville's administration and way of life at the beginning of the twelfth century. The city was governed by the officers that usually controlled the cities of Spanish Islam: the *cadi* or civil judge, the *sahib al-medina* or governor, the *muhtasib* or market-inspector, to mention only a few. A treatise by al-Tudjibi gives details of the way in which Seville was governed, including the frailties of the civil servants. The document also provides information about the affairs of the old mosque, which was already being found inadequate for the quickly growing population; it tells of the two imams, the many muezzins, the architect, the water-carriers and the various acolytes; the outer precincts of the mosque teeming with merchants, beggars and beasts of burden. In the many smaller mosques of the city, primary classes were given by teachers, many of whom were neither very learned nor over-zealous in performing their duties. The Moslem graveyards were the scene of scandalous goings-on: there were attempted seductions of the women who visited them; mountebanks used to practise fortune-telling there; even leather-tanners would use the tombstones to spread out their hides in the sun.

The River Guadalquivir presented a lively scene: the port bustled with trading ships and the river was filled with the boats that ferried passengers and merchandise to the opposite bank, for at that time there was no bridge. Higher up the river, the water-carriers drew the water that they later sold in the city; no aqueduct

31. Part of the Patio de las Doncellas in the Alcázar of Seville. The courtyard has foiled arches supported on double columns; the walls are covered in tiles and *attawriq* decoration.

32. The Patio del Yeso, adjoining the Almohad outer wall of the Alcázar of Seville. One of the few remaining examples of genuine Arabic architecture in the Alcázar, most of which is Mudejar.

was built to supply Seville with fresh water until the Almohad period. At the city gates the officials collected the unpopular local excise-duties, and it was difficult to know whether the veiled passers-by were really Almoravids, or slaves or wrongdoers passing themselves off as Africans. The markets were full of meat, vegetables, figs, melons, olive-oil, spices, fried fish and other titbits; the bakers made bread from the customers' own flour.

If one could have wandered through Moorish Seville, one would have seen the incredible variety of craftsmen at work: masons and carpenters, potters and glass-makers, blacksmiths and farriers, basket-weavers, mat-makers and esparto-workers, weavers and dyers, furriers and tanners, tailors and shoemakers, manufacturers of parchment and paper, joiners and cabinet-makers, tilers and brick-makers. Everywhere, one would have come across fortune-tellers, ballad-singers, and butchers carrying carcasses of meat from the slaughterhouses to the markets. There would have been many physicians and apothecaries, as well as a considerable number of prostitutes. There were also public baths, with barbers and masseurs in attendance, and Christian churches, though among the Moslems it was not thought proper to enter the latter. All this detail is to be found in al-Tudjibi's work. Of the Christian churches, he declares:

" Moslem women should be forbidden to enter them, because the priests are a pack of libertines, adulterers and debauchees. Women should only be allowed there at festivals and on days of collective prayer, for at other times they drink, eat and fornicate with the priests, each of whom spends the night with two or even more of these women. This has become the usual custom of these clerics; they have made licit acts that are illicit. They should be obliged to marry, as they are in the East, or at least allowed to do so if they wish. If they refuse to take a wife, it should then be illegal for any woman, young or old, to enter a priest's house. They should be forced to circumcise themselves, as Jesus (may he be exalted!) was circumcised. They hold a festival to celebrate his circumcision but they do not emulate him."

Speaking of the duties of the police and the night patrol, al-Tudjibi asserts:

" Their evidence should not be valid unless corroborated by that of the townspeople. Measures should be taken against those officers that are corrupt or drunken, for there is nothing worse than that they should break the regulations, yet many of them do so. Similar steps should be taken against all the employees of the city governor when they fail in their duty to make enquiries, both in the daytime and at night, for such enquiry would unveil a great deal. Anyone found abroad at night should be taken to his dwelling, without his necessarily being suspected of evildoing. If a man is arrested at night, the patrol should not take any of his property or remove his clothes; he should be brought before the city governor the next morning in the state in which he was found. The night patrols have an unpleasant habit of stealing clothes, removing possessions and intimidating people. If they take up a man and wish to keep him in custody, they should place him in a lodging-house, in the care of the proprietor until the next day. The patrols should make a number of rounds each night and vary their beats, because the thieves and criminals watch out for the patrol before committing their misdemeanours and felonies. Criminals should be promptly tried and rigorously punished, for their objectives are murder and robbery."

All al-Tudjibi's criticisms are made in the same bitter and immoderate tone; even so, he gives us a detailed picture of the habits and outlook of the Almoravid period of Seville.

33. The wrought-iron door of the Banqueting Hall in the Alcázar of Seville. The elaborate ornamentation around the door is characteristic of Mudejar workmanship.

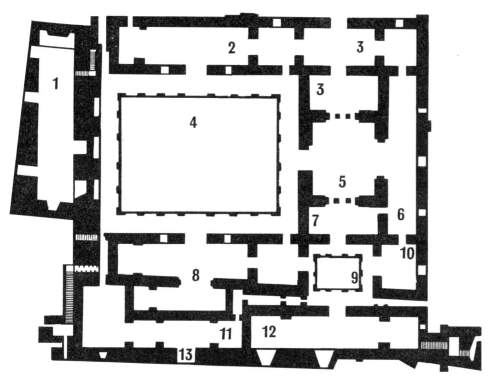

PLAN OF THE ALCÁZAR AT SEVILLE

1 Chapel
2 Salón de Carlos V (Hall of Charles V)
3 Aposentos de la Padilla (Padilla Apartments)
4 Patio de las Doncellas (Courtyard of the Maidens)
5 Salón de los Embajadores (Hall of the Ambassadors)
6 Comedor de Felipe II (Dining-hall of Philip II)
7 Sala de Felipe II (Hall of Philip II)
8 Dormitorio de los Reyes Moros (Sleeping-quarters of the Moorish Kings)
9 Patio de las Muñecas (Courtyard of the Dolls)
10 Sala de los Reyes Católicos (Hall of the Catholic Kings)
11 Entrance-hall
12 Salón de los Príncipes (Hall of the Princes)
13 Puerta del León (Gate of the Lion)

The Giralda and the Alcázar

The best period for art in Moslem Seville was in the reigns of the first Almohad monarchs. Very little now remains of their art and architecture, because the Christians built over their constructions. The minarets of some of their mosques can still be seen incorporated in the towers of the Churches of St Catherine and St Mark, and above all in the Cathedral (once the great mosque), from which rises the magnificent Giralda.

The Giralda (*ill.* 29) is the most popular monument in Seville and one of the best known of all Spanish buildings. Originally the minaret of the great Mosque in Seville, it was built to commemorate the victory of the Almohads at Alarcos and was finished in 1197. One of its chief *alarifes* or architects was Ahmad ben Baso. When the Christians entered Seville during the Reconquest, they expressed great admiration for this tower. It is said that when the conquered Moors asked Prince Alfonso the Wise (later King Alfonso X) if they could demolish the tower, he replied that " if they removed a single stone, they would all be put to the sword." Giralda, the name by which it is now known, has nothing to do with Arabic: it derives from a colossal bronze statue of Faith, of the sixteenth century, which serves as a weather-vane (hence *giralda*) and tops the belfry that in 1568 replaced the original small tower crowned by four golden balls. The minaret in its early form was very similar to the Hassan Tower in Rabat and the Djami al-Kutubiyin in Marrakesh of which it was the prototype. The gigantic tower stands nearly 230 feet high (almost 328 feet counting the Renaissance additions), and is 44 feet square. The matt, but clean state of the ochre of its bricks is due to the restoration undertaken at the end of the nineteenth century. In order to ensure the solidity of a building constructed in this material, the walls are over eight feet thick. Because of this, the interior is surprisingly cool in summer. A little light comes in from the windows, of which the lower ones are single and the remainder composed of coupled arches with dividing pillars, decorated with arabesques. The interior is not decorated. The tower is climbed by a ramp made of bricks placed on end, permitting the top to be reached on horse-back. The conqueror of the city, King Ferdinand the Saint, is said to have ascended the tower in this fashion. The ramp rises by right-angled turns with thirty-four numbered landings, finally reaching the platform. Then there is an additional ramp leading to the Christian belfry. It is well worth making the ascent to obtain a bird's-eye-view of the city, which is circular and compact, broken by the myriad zigzags of its streets. One can see, too, the Moorish character of old Seville. But if one looks straight down at the roofs of the adjoining Cathedral and the Patio de los Naranjos, one loses the sensation that the Giralda was originally a Moslem minaret.

Another ancient Almohad monument in Seville, the Alcázar, is equally disillusioning. Not even in its most Moorish parts does one gain the impression of strolling through an Arab palace. But such it was, built in the twelfth century, no doubt on the site of the ancient acropolis. The Patio de las Doncellas in this palace recalls the tribute of a hundred girls that the Moorish king used to exact from the Christians for his harem. In contrast to the Alhambra, which has an immediate charm, in the Alcázar of Seville everything is artificial except what is modern. This is because the palace became the residence of the Christian kings after the Reconquest, and many alterations were made. In addition, many fires and earth tremors contributed to the destruction of the original building. It is difficult now to disentangle the complexity of constructions that went into its

36

Coming Home from the Fair, by Gustave Doré.

making. Actually, the oldest parts of the present structure seem to date from the fourteenth century. They are the work of Pedro I (known to history both as Peter the Cruel and Peter the Just), of all the Spanish monarchs the one who most felt he belonged to Seville. Everything in Seville evokes memories of him: the old Jewish quarter, now the suburb of Santa Cruz, where he used to stroll and have love-affairs and quarrels; the legends of the justice he administered or the crimes he committed. Almost all that is Moorish in the Alcázar today is the work of this monarch and therefore must be considered Mudejar.

Mudejar art was fostered by some Christian princes who wished to have palaces built in Arabic style and who had Moslem craftsmen brought to their courts. In reality it is a mixed art in which Romanesque and later Gothic influences are added to the typical Arabic designs and material. These craftsmen had a great command of structure and even the Cistercian monks had recourse to them on more than one occasion. The decoration is extremely complex and uses all kinds of design. The materials used are brick, wood and plaster, which were unknown to the Christians at the time when the Mudejars were building.

Of all the styles of Spanish Moslem art, it is the Nasrid art of Granada which has survived best and which best evokes a civilization and a culture that were strangely sophisticated and particularly captivating. It is with this art that we shall be dealing in the next chapters.

37. Some of the roofs of the Royal Palace of the Alhambra at Granada.

38. The cupola of the Salón de los Embajadores, also known as the Sala de Comares, in the Serrallo of the Alhambra. This cupola is of the *media naranja* type, resembling four segments of a halved orange, executed in *lacería*, or " carpentry of knots "; the arms of Castile and León were added to the decoration by the Christian conquerors.

39. (*p.* 95) Balcony in the Salón de los Embajadores at the Alhambra, overlooking the Peinador de la Reina. The inscription surrounding the foiled arch reads—" Only God is the conqueror."

40. (*p.* 96) The Torre de Comares in the Alhambra; adjoining it, the galleries of the rooms occupied by the Holy Roman Emperor Charles V.

93

Genealogical Table of the Abbadid Dynasty of Seville

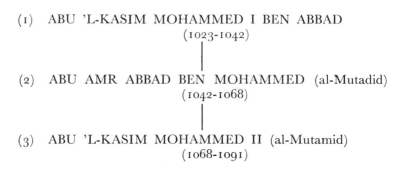

(1)   ABU 'L-KASIM MOHAMMED I BEN ABBAD
(1023-1042)

(2)   ABU AMR ABBAD BEN MOHAMMED (al-Mutadid)
(1042-1068)

(3)   ABU 'L-KASIM MOHAMMED II (al-Mutamid)
(1068-1091)

Al-Mutamid was deposed by the Almoravids in 1091 and Seville was governed by the Almoravid general, Sir, on behalf of the Almoravid Sultans of the Maghrib. In 1147, Barraz ben Mohammed al-Masufi, general of the Almohad Sultan Abd al-Mumin, captured Seville from the Almoravids. In the reign of Abu Yakub Yusuf (1163-1184), Seville became the Almohad headquarters in Spain. In 1228, Seville fell into the hands of the rebel Mohammed ben Yusuf ben Hud, who finally drove the Almohads out of Spain. King Ferdinand III of Castile and León captured Seville from the Moors in 1248 after a siege that lasted sixteen months.

GRANADA

Alhambra, ciudad del agua
regalo de Alá
puerta del Paraíso...

Anon.

GRANADA'S NOSTALGIC MAJESTY

THERE SEEMS TO BE a law governing men's evolutionary process according to which political decadence results in a great flowering of art and culture. Granada was no exception to this. The decadence of the Spanish Islamic Empire, with its territorial, religious and political disintegration, led without interruption to the late splendour of the Kingdom of Granada. The earlier warlike spirit of the Andalusian Moslems was replaced by a growing tendency for luxury and delicacy and for the ultimate refinements of physical and mental pleasure. The former Syrian or Berber chieftains were succeeded by monarchs with cultured and sumptuous courts, where their nostalgia for their lost political power was soothed by music, poetry and the minor domestic arts, to which they devoted themselves without any thought for the future. The fortresses that long before had marked the boundary between the Christian and Moslem worlds had slowly crumbled away, and on their ruins were built filigreed structures of fragile materials. The peoples who had earlier triumphed and imposed their customs and much of their character and religious faith on a large section of the conquered, were themselves now undergoing a change, and, convinced of their own decline, were becoming sceptical. Yet it was then that Granada suddenly entered its best and liveliest mood—a mood that thrived on a sense of crisis and transition, on a feeling of having reached a crossroads.

From the early tribes of Iberia through the Roman Empire, Islam, the Renaissance and Baroque periods, every stage of Spanish history is represented, sometimes very fully, in Granada's shining streets, in the buildings of many periods and in the customs that are still followed with surprisingly little change. Of all these successive influences, the most intense and far-reaching was clearly that of Islam. Yet there is something more: something indefinable that goes much deeper, that one breathes in the sparkling air that comes down from the snowy peaks of the Sierra to the myrtles of the plain; something that pervades the sonorous peace of the gardens and emanates from both the old and the new buildings; above all, something that can be sensed in the sad eyes and the soft, singing voices of the people of Granada. It is this that we can call the city's essential spirit; or, as one of Granada's greatest writers of the last century, Ángel Ganivet, expressed it, the " diamond hub " of the city.

Granada is a city that cannot be defined or explained by comparison with other cities. There is no common denominator for the purpose, nor can one rely on the evolution of Oriental and Western architectural styles. There are other

99

Spanish cities brimming over with relics of a glorious past; but in none of them does history endure in such a lively and palpable way as it does in Granada. Seville is more bustling, more frolicsome, more picturesque on the surface. Cordoba, solemn and silent, looks back on a vast and dominating history. Toledo is an outstanding example of a well-preserved ancient city. The same can be said of Ávila, Salamanca, Santiago de Compostela, Cáceres and many more. Yet, in all these cities the past is dead and brings scarcely any influence to bear on the present. Granada is different: there it seems as though all the cultural influences that arrived and became rooted in the city marked it indelibly with an absolute character, intermingling to produce a peculiar code of living and behaviour which has no equal anywhere else.

It is also impossible to explain Granada in the same way as Toledo or Constantinople, as the result of a balance between East and West, which were in contact in those cities for many centuries. There, divers cultures have brought about a complex mixture, whose parts can be recognized and isolated. In Granada, on the contrary, this type of analysis will not prove very useful. The various peoples who have lived in it and enlarged and improved it were not the only determinants of the modern city. One of the finest expositors of Granada, Prieto-Moreno, mentions the main determining factors: the geographical position, the vegetation, the climate and the scenery. Throughout history these factors moulded the peculiar character of the inhabitants, whatever their origin, and also shaped their thinking, their customs and their art. Here, too, lie the clues which will lead the visitor to Granada to understand the city fully.

Federico García Lorca, the best known of all Granada's sons, as much for his writing as for the tragic circumstances surrounding his death, once said that Granada " cannot leave its home ". Indeed, the ancient city of the sultans has no horizons that promise a life of adventure. The city is home-loving and self-absorbed, and its inhabitants are engrossed in their surroundings in a silent, serene manner that borders on mysticism. Modern life, with its dynamic flurry and demented haste, holds no attractions for them. On the contrary, they find themselves more attracted to the contemplative side of life, to artistic pastimes at home, to music and to gazing at the surrounding scenery. Granada's aesthetic outlook is preoccupied with minute and exquisite things. Friar Luis de Granada, one of the city's great classical writers, said in his *Introduction to the Symbol of Faith* that Divine Providence shines out brightest and best from things that are small and simple rather than from spectacular and grandiose things. It is as though Granada would prefer to shut itself up in its alcoves and workshops to work on its filigreed ivory, its tapestries and embroidery, its marquetry and wrought copper, amid the delicate gurgling of the fountains and the familiar scent of the myrtles, whose perfume pervades the city; when these trees are coated with the dust of noon, they emit an acrid hot smell, but in the dusk, when they are watered by the dew, their fragrance becomes velvety and smooth, an aroma that is delicately erotic and almost without equal.

Despite the large renaissance and baroque structures and the lofty fortifying walls, Granada's setting has been planned in a neat, domestic manner. The chief natural features are given less importance than the fruit-baskets and flower-garlands arranged by the city's housewives. Here, leisure does not consist of doing nothing; rather, it has an intimate, spiritual bent, and becomes a static absorption in fantasy and contemplation. All the inhabitants of Granada like to gaze at the water that is to be found everywhere in the city and at the cool,

41. Slender columns in the Patio de los Leones at the Alhambra support arches decorated with *mocárabe*, or stalactite, plaster-work.

42. The Patio de los Leones at the Alhambra, showing the crudely hewn lions that contrast sharply with the sophisticated ornamentation of the arches.

subtle twilights. They are not troubled by the splendour of their natural surroundings. They choose to stay at home, or chat quietly in the clubs and cafés, watching the rain falling or the sun glinting on the pavements. They are a reserved people, little given to noisy excitement, except for the gipsies of the Sacromonte, with their sophisticated *zambras*. They are not hurried or overworked or ambitious. They are content with what they have, which is not inconsiderable. Granada's tranquillity encourages daydreaming; it is inclined more to the plastic than to the philosophic; to lyricism than to drama. Its true personality lurks inside its houses, in its peaceful scenery and in the gurgling sound of its streams, full of a strange, noble nostalgia, which recalls the city's melancholy Nasrid rulers; this personality is wafted down from the tiny balconies and slips out through the curtains of an open window. In a fine passage, Lorca describes Granada thus:

" It is completely different from Seville. Seville is man with his sensual and sentimental complexes. It represents political intrigue and the triumphal arch. King Pedro and Don Juan. It is full of the human element and its voice draws tears, because everyone can understand it. Granada is like the story of what happened in Seville. There is a lack of anything that is definitely finished... From the outside, everything has a soft, domestic air; but who can really penetrate this intimacy? When in the seventeenth century a poet of Granada, Pedro Soto de Rojas, returned from Madrid full of sadness and disillusion, he wrote a work entitled *A Paradise closed to many, gardens open to all*; it seems to me that here he exactly defined Granada, ' a paradise closed to many'."

The contemplative people of Granada take pleasure in domestic arts and crafts, especially music and painting; there is hardly a *carmen*, as the houses built by Christians in Granada are called, without its guitar and its painter's easel. There is no question of professionalism; virtually all the citizens are amateurs of these arts. Because of this, they cannot be judged by one criterion, for they possess strong individuality and are incapable of mass-thinking or mass-action. Their introspective tendency is reflected in their houses, at least in those that have not been modernized. The central element of these dwellings is the *patio*, which serves as reception-room, living-room and drawing-room. Gómez Moreno says that the *patio* in Granada performs " the function of insulation from the outside world, without losing contact with nature, which is represented in it by many plants and pots of flowers, not forgetting the water of the fountain, which takes on a ritualistic role. All the literary gatherings, *tertulias*, parties and *fiestas*, typical of Granada, take place in the *patio*, and its influence makes itself felt on the gardens and on the whole of the city on such occasions as the Feast of Corpus Christi, when the house-fronts are decorated with quilts and copper pans, the streets are covered over with canvas awnings, and the ground spread with sweet-smelling rushes. If the builder had sufficient space, the house will have a kitchen-garden or a yard, which despite their utilitarian purpose, will be pleasant places. In the larger houses, the garden will have vegetables as well as flowers, and even fruit-trees. Between the house and the kitchen-garden, there will be a series of tiny gardens, which become successively more intimate, leading to the favourite spots for summer and winter. The different stages of this lay-out follow an authentically Oriental sense of fusing the pleasure-garden and the kitchen-garden. Both *patio* and garden provide pleasant settings for the *tertulias*, at which witty conversation is the rule in the spirit of Granada's quietly intellectual atmosphere and its inhabitants' keen critical sense. The

43. Detail of the floral and geometric decoration on the capitals in the Patio de los Leones.

105

gatherings often leave the *cármenes* to stroll, stopping all conversation fom time to time to admire the sunset. These literary *tertulias* go back to the '98 Generation of writers, 'the Granada group', who gathered around Ángel Ganivet at the Avellano Fountain."

When Gautier and Washington Irving reached the walls of the Alhambra, Granada was still a city in utter isolation, and its customs had been formed in a mould that was still intact and uncontaminated by other urban centres; the city was, therefore, full of history and legend. Even today, there are many picturesque details to be observed in the streets and houses of Granada; there are many survivals of the habits of Islam. In some of the city's taverns there is still segregation of the sexes, as though the days of the harem and the gynaeceum were not forgotten. And there are still the gipsies, of obscure origin, perhaps from Egypt or India, and on hot afternoons the water-sellers continue to proffer their refreshing liquid for very little payment. They draw this water from one of the many fountains, such as the Avellano, mentioned above, hidden in the twisting gorge of the Darro, where Ángel Ganivet used to invite to a countryside *tertulia* the friends who shared his desire to make Granada a cultural and intellectual centre.

The plan of modern Granada presents a varied and confused appearance. As much by their atmosphere as by their topographical position, the various suburbs seem to be separate towns. But in Granada it is not topography that will explain the urban development; rather it is the movement of history, which caused new suburbs to spring up and produced an unusual urban mass, whose lay-out seems to be neither logical nor justifiable. The streets are scattered across the plain and over the hills from two noticeable nuclei: the upper city and the lower city. The former encloses the latter and stretches over an alluvial embankment down to the Vega. This upper area is spread over several hills, the red colour of which probably explains the name of the Alhambra (*hamra* being the Arabic for " crimson "). These hills, which are separated by the gorges of the Darro and the Genil, are the remains of an ancient cone of debris that overlay the mountainous edges of the Granada basin. On the descent from the towers of the Alhambra down the slope of the Rey Chico, a ravine runs down from the Generalife to the Darro with the red silt and the crimson palaces gleaming amid the dense greenery. The hills break up the views and create perspectives.

* * *

In spite of its insular and rather provincial character, Granada has never failed to influence the course of Spanish history, sometimes decisively. Evidence of this is provided by such of the city's institutions as the Archbishop's Palace, where the ghost of Hernando de Talavera, Queen Isabella's confessor, still seems to lurk; the headquarters of the Captaincy General, the founding of which recalls the energetic Marquis of Mondéjar—the post being later held by the Great Captain, Gonzalo de Córdoba; the modern Audiencia Territorial or regional court which replaced the ancient Chancery of Granada; and the University, successor of the Moorish cultural institutions, which continues to supply both Spain and Europe with eminent men of learning.

Gipsies Dancing at the Sacromonte, by Gustave Doré.

107

Unlike Cordoba, Granada was never the capital or heart of a powerful empire. On the contrary, its splendid and glorious past was always associated with political decadence and depended on kingdoms with little capacity for expansion. This perhaps accounts for the hypersensitive spirit and intellectual disposition of its inhabitants, for both these tendencies usually go hand in hand with the historical decline of a people who have earlier been triumphant rulers. When the epic dies away, lyric poetry quivers into being; when swords are consigned to the armoury, art and culture begin to unfurl themselves in the mellow peace that the swords have wrought.

The historical destiny of Granada was clearly determined by a topographical, or rather, strategic peculiarity: although the city lies close to a sea-coast particularly prone to invasion, it is surrounded and protected by a compact chain of mountains. In consequence of this natural phenomenon all the foreign peoples who managed to capture the city settled there in comparative safety, relying on the apparent ease with which they could defend themselves against further invaders. Indeed, the physical geography of Granada is a world in miniature where all the topographical irregularities seem to be concentrated in a very small space: the highest range of mountains in Spain descends abruptly to a fertile plain, while just beyond lies a coastal belt covered with semi-tropical vegetation.

It would be difficult to find a city and a countryside richer in geographical contrasts. The city lies on the lower slopes of the Sierra Nevada, or rather, at the foot of that range, between the two hills surmounted by the Alhambra and the Albaicín quarter, which are separated by the gorge of the River Darro. Both these hills overlook the wide Vega or plain, which is crossed by Granada's second river, the Genil. In the background rise the snow-covered peaks of the Sierra. The range was probably once a single, continuous rocky mass, only later split up by streams and rivers. This division produced a series of smaller hills, some isolated, some part of a chain which includes those now known as San Cristóbal, the Albaicín, the Alhambra and Los Mártires, all four flanking the city. To the south-west of Granada extends the Vega, extremely fertile country dotted with small villages. Well-watered and bathed in sunlight for most of the year, the Vega has a very mild climate. It is protected from strong winds by a series of mountain ranges which include the Sierra Nevada, the Sierra de Alhama, the Sierra de Loja, the Sierra de Parapanda, the Sierra de Motril and the Sierra de Cogollos.

The River Darro, known to the Moslems as the *Hadarro*, runs through a gorge that separates the hills of the Sacromonte and Albaicín quarters from the Alhambra hill, flows through the city, and joins the Genil. The Genil, known to the Romans as the *Singili* and to the Arabs as the *Chingil*, flows through leafy groves to the Vega, which it irrigates, and then rolls on to join the Guadalquivir some miles beyond.

One important point that often passes unnoticed is that the city, since it faces west, receives quite a considerable amount of rain from the Atlantic, through the gap in the hills near the lower Guadalquivir; this rainfall is less than that of Cordoba but almost as great as Seville's. This source of water, together with the many rivers swollen by the snow of the Sierra, provides the Vega with natural irrigation, which rarely has to be regulated by the inhabitants. The resulting harvests, which are rich and varied, grown in the mud left by the rivers in spate, have always provided a reliable source of food. They were only found lacking in the fifteenth century, when the Christian onrush drove waves of refugees into Granada, until its population reached a total of 200,000 inhabitants, as many as it has today. It was at that time that the Sultan Ismail, father of Abu ' l-Hasan Ali, ordered that the surrounding hill should be tilled and irrigated by means of costly aqueducts bringing over the waters of the Darro.

The Gipsies' Quarter in Granada, by Gustave Doré.

The Sultanate thus had supplementary crops at its disposal, safe from the hostile incursions of the Castilians. Granada is really full of water: it fills the air with its cool sounds and makes the land fertile.

Early History

Amidst this unusual and magnificent natural scene, each of the cultures that came or was brought to Spain ran its proud course. It is clear that men of the bronze and iron ages must have set foot on these coasts and sought the mineral deposits of the interior. It was these minerals that, centuries later, were to attract and quicken the greed of the Phoenician merchantmen who founded their first trading-posts at the township now known as Almuñécar, which was then the last port of call on the long voyage to Gades (Cadiz). It was on the stretch of the Mediterranean near Granada that Homer sang, through the lips of bold Odysseus, of the wine-dark sea, when the Greeks challenged the Tyrian hegemony.

The Phoenicians and Greeks must have discovered the first of the Tartessian tribes, the Turduli, settled in the hills of Granada. According to historians, they were the most civilized of all the tribes of ancient Iberia. It appears that Granada had its origin as the dwelling-place of the Turduli. It was in their time that Hecataeus of Miletus mentioned the city which he called *Elybirge* or *Elubirge*. On contemporary coins the sun symbol was depicted and the Iberian name of *Iliverri*, which the historian Humboldt interpreted as "new city", was inscribed.

But if these remote antecedents left few physical traces or monuments among the hills where present-day Granada stands, those bequeathed by Rome and its Empire were many and important. To the universal city of Latium the Spanish city owes the power of cohesion so characteristic of that greatest empire of antiquity. The bridges that cross its various rivers, the highways that connect the city with the coast and the interior, all bear witness to the presence of the Romans, as does the basic outline of an irrigation system that, later, at the peak of Islamic splendour, was to be fully developed and expanded by the Moslems. Under the ægis of the Romans, Granada continued minting coins on which, in Latin characters, the name *Eliber, Eliberri, Iliberri* etc. is inscribed. In referring to this period, Ptolemy calls the city *Illiberi*, while Pliny the Elder names it *Illiberri* and its citizens *Liberini*. The Romans designated as a *municipium* of their Empire the township that was to become the city of the Sultans of the Nasrid Dynasty. Inscriptions from the third to the first centuries B.C. call the town *Municipium Florentinum Iliberitanum* and sometimes *Florentia*, names that seem to mean something like the "flowering" or "fruitful" city. This town, which was important in its time, was centred on the area which now consists of the suburbs of the Alcazaba and the Albaicín, where remains of Roman buildings have been found. The extent of these ruins illustrates the prestige of that community; it is also shown by the fact that St Cecil was sent there in 62 A.D.; the saint established his episcopal see in the town that was to become Granada and made it the centre of his preachings. Years later, some time between 302 and 304, it was the scene of a most important theological meeting, the first Spanish council of the Catholic Church.

At the beginning of the Dark Ages, when the Germanic hordes invaded the Iberian Peninsula, one of the tribes, the Swabians, reached the lands of Granada, which they conquered after a long and dauntless struggle in which they had to overcome not only the wild and difficult Andalusian mountains, but also and especially the stubborn resistance of the local tribes using guerrilla methods, tactics that have been frequently practised throughout Spanish history. Once the territory had been subdued and the Visigothic Monarchy established over most of the Peninsula, Illiberis continued through the sixth century to enjoy its importance as a fortified town of outstanding strategic value, as the architectural finds in the oldest part of the Alcazaba have demonstrated. In that period Granada retained its ancient rank as capital of a province, increasing in importance with its growing military value and with the decline of other towns in the neighbourhood, such as Castilia, which lay in an enclave near Atarfe on the slopes of the range later to be known as Elvira.

Near the hill on which Illiberis was growing in the Visigothic period, stood a second town, hidden among the slopes that stretch from the Alhambra to the River Genil and inhabited by Jews. This ghetto was called *Garnatha Alyehud* and it is from this name that some historians derive the name Granada. Of the numerous speculations this etymology appears to be the most likely.

It has been said that it was the Jews living in Garnatha or Garnata in 711 A.D.

—the date of the first Moslem invasion of the Peninsula—who enabled the Moorish leader Tarik to enter the precincts of the city, motivated by their eternal religious rivalries with the Christians who at that time inhabited the opposite hill of Illiberis. The name Granada was adopted by the Moslems when some Moors from Syria settled in the city—some of the few authentic Arabs who came to Spain, the majority of the Moslem invaders being Berbers from North Africa.

The Moors

The true history of Granada, or at least that part of it which has been preserved most brilliantly and has left the deepest mark, began with the fall of the Visigothic Monarchy in the face of the frenzied sweep of the Moslem wave. The first glimpse of that vegetation, climate, panorama of snow and running water, must have taken away the breath of those desert nomads. The consequence, as an historian of Granada has pointed out, was that the destructive spirit of the nomadic warriors, now settled amid that fine landscape of mountain and plain on hills that seemed to form a vast garden, underwent a steadying transformation, finally giving way to the peaceful, poetic and particularly contemplative nature characteristic of the people of the Nasrid Dynasty.

Before this, however, the city went through a confused period of violence and treachery. This was the time of the *taifa* kingdoms. Granada was the setting for many of the internal religious and racial struggles of the Moslems and the troubles that followed the death of al-Mansur and the collapse of the Caliphate. Castilia, the ancient capital of the Elvira Kingdom, was destroyed in 1010 in one of these turmoils and the rulers of that kingdom looked towards Granada as a possible new capital. It was a Berber dynasty that finally conferred this honour on the city: Zawi ben Ziri, first of the Zirids, founded the kingdom that was to maintain that status for the next four centuries.

The Zirids ruled throughout the eleventh century and provided four monarchs: Zawi, the founder of the dynasty, Habbus, Badis and Abd Allah. It was Habbus who transferred his Court to the new capital and began enlarging the city. This enlargement continued in the reign of Badis, who improved the fortifications of the hill called Sabika, on which the Alhambra now stands, and built a sumptuous palace on the ruins of the Roman fort known as the Alcazaba, as well as other buildings that increased the city's perimeter. Abd Allah embellished the city even more, but in 1090 it was demolished during the Almoravid invasion. Under the Almoravids and the Almohads who followed them, the city continued to be enlarged and beautified, and many mosques and schools were built. After the defeat of the Almohads at Las Navas de Tolosa in 1212, a descendant of the Moorish kings of Saragossa called Banu Hud wrested Granada from the last of the North Africans and proclaimed himself Emir. It was then that Mohammed Banu 'l-Ahmar emerged. With the ending of the Berber domination of Granada, the connection with true Arab stock was renewed. The Spanish Moors were then to remain on Peninsular soil for two long centuries.

The most magnificent period of Granada's history was achieved by the efforts of a pure-blooded Arab family, the Banu Nasrs of Arjona, who were to provide a new and lasting contribution to the permanence of Islam in al-Andalus. Under their rule, Granada was to display to advantage the heritage bequeathed to it by the earlier Umayyad Empire, and its first ruler, Abu Abd Allah Mohammed Banu 'l-Ahmar, bestowed on Granada the sparkling and beguiling appearance that still astonishes and thrills us today.

In the warm and blossoming May of 1238, Banu 'l-Ahmar led his army to the top of Sabika, the bright red hill on which a century before the Berber Zawi had set foot, homesick for his oases in the Maghrib. Banu 'l-Ahmar's aims were as noble as his origins. He was cultured and seems to have had a clear idea of his destiny as a great king of a decadent nation. He soon began to demonstrate his firm resolve: a few months after his accession to the throne of Granada, a large part of al-Andalus agreed to pay tributes to him. Upon the red stone Alcazaba of the Zirids that lay in ruins on the hill overlooking the luxuriant plain and the shimmering narrows of the River Darro, the new Sultan began the construction of the finest of all Moorish al-kasrs. The work was to take two centuries. Halls, water channels and gardens followed one another in slow succession as the Alhambra grew under the tender attentions of the twenty Nasrid monarchs. The enclosure, still encircled by the venerable and by that time almost useless walls, was enlarged and embellished under the expert care of Banu 'l-Ahmar's son and successor, Mohammed II, and especially under that of the two greatest royal builders of the Dynasty: Yusuf I, who constructed many of the towers and rooms that still survive, such as the Casa Real and the Baño Regio; and Mohammed V, who brought the great enterprise to completion.

It was, however, the founder of the Nasrid Dynasty (the last reigning Moslem dynasty in Spain), Banu 'l-Ahmar of Arjona, who was the real creator of this palace, which, as Hernando del Pulgar was to comment when the Christians first set foot in Granada, " can rather be regarded as a city in itself than as a fortress or a royal palace ", so numerous were its halls, rooms, courtyards and gardens. If we ventured to define Banu 'l-Ahmar's constructional policy in very modern terms, we could say that it was essentially hydraulic; it was as though his obsession with water was an atavistic impulse inherited from his desert ancestors. It was he who ordered the construction of the water-course called the Acequia Real, that bore the golden water of the Darro over more than a league and carried it skilfully up the then bare sides of Sabika to the very heart of the incipient Alhambra. This water-course was and still is the life-blood of the palace and its gardens: it has made possible the outstandingly beautiful blending of stucco and vegetation, the combination of cool, shaded porches and secluded arbours. Nowhere else in the whole history of architecture has such a skilful and perfect harmony been created, of buildings, gardens, fountains and water-traps.

Mohammed Banu 'l-Ahmar first saw the clear light of the Southern day in Arjona in the year 581 of the Moslem Hegira (1195 A.D.). His parents, perhaps foreseeing a wealthy and important future for their offspring, provided him with a sophisticated education and instilled in him a noble ambition, an authoritarian dignity and a thirst for greatness. He absorbed the whole mass of Moslem artistic, religious and scientific knowledge, as well as the more fixed European university disciplines of the *trivium* and the *quadrivium*. While still a youth, Banu 'l-Ahmar was appointed governor of Arjona and Jaén, because he was already extremely popular both with his own people and with those who were later to be his subjects. They all began to place in him a trust that had earlier been constantly broken by the weakness, cruelty and stupidity of their former rulers. Indeed, the internal squabbles of the latter and the further disintegration of the *taifas* into smaller fragments were favourable to Banu 'l-Ahmar's rise to power. When Banu Hud died, the Moslems of al-Andalus became even more divided and many cities, left without any form of government, declared themselves for Banu 'l-Ahmar, who was not slow to accept the power that was offered him almost unanimously.

44. Leaf of a door in carved wood in the Patio de los Leones at the Alhambra.

45. The Patio de los Arrayanes at the Alhambra.

His moderate outlook, his courage and his deep rooted ambition brought him to the forefront throughout the Moslem lands amid popular acclaim. Cities, fortresses and towns vied with one another to hail him until he finally came to the greatly desired throne of the Zirids in the city he saw as his real goal, which was then on the point of falling forlornly into rack and ruin. His triumph was at hand. The throne of Granada loomed before him and he climbed its steps with due solemnity. He did not pass down them again until his death, more than thirty years later.

Banu 'l-Ahmar's reign began propitiously. There are many contemporary accounts of his beneficent rule. A later historian who gathered together these accounts tells us that his reign was one of constant prosperity. Even if we discount much of this as romantic adulation, we are faced by the fact that all the documents of the period bear witness to his skill in governing. In the various cities of his kingdom he delegated authority to those chieftains and loyal members of his household who had the knack of keeping public order on the one hand, and who possessed, on the other, that combination of courage and prudence that recommended itself to the king. He also organized an alert police force and administered justice by means of extremely strict laws created by new *alfaquíes*, laws that were typical of his brand of paternalistic tyranny. Humble and unfortunate people were most protected by his legislation; they were never denied the right of a palace audience and furthermore, it is known that the monarch provided assistance from his private funds, as well as from the public exchequer, to help the needy. He also set up homes for the blind and the aged, hospitals for all types of invalids, hospices and similar establishments. But the king did not confine himself merely to founding such institutions; from time to time he would visit them. It is said that his visits were made " not on previously appointed days and with ceremony, so that everything would seem to be conducted properly with all the abuses well hidden, rather the king would arrive suddenly when he was least expected and enquire personally of the way in which the sick and homeless were treated by those put in charge of them. "

Banu 'l-Ahmar was equally devoted to the education of his subjects. He created numerous centres of learning in which all the knowledge of the epoch was taught. He also established an efficient system of public supplies and trading, setting up meat and bread depôts where the people could obtain these vital commodities at fair and fixed prices. He had a good water supply laid in the city and many public fountains and baths installed, in addition to the numerous aqueducts and watercourses that irrigated and enriched the naturally fertile plain. " In this fashion," one chronicler tells us, " the fine city was filled with abundance and prosperity, its gates were open to commerce and industry and its shops were full of merchandise from all over the world. "

It seems that about a hundred and fifty thousand people inhabited the hills and plain of Granada at that time. When the continuous struggles of the Berbers had ceased, they appear to have enjoyed peace and prosperity until one day Banu 'l-Ahmar himself became inextricably involved in new and violent conflicts. The increasingly powerful armies of Castile and Aragon now dedicated themselves to the arduous task of reconquering their lost territories and they had already recovered a large part of al-Andalus. Jaime I had occupied Valencia, while Ferdinand III, the Saint, was leading his triumphant hosts across most of Andalusia. It was when the Castilian King Ferdinand held under tight siege the city of Jaén, one of the jewels of the Nasrid Crown, that Banu 'l-Ahmar came to

46. One of the few remaining parts of the Alhambra Mosque; this small tower once housed the *mihrab*.

observe his complete lack of retaliatory power in the face of an attack by the
Castilians who were tough and well equipped fighters, accustomed to long mar-
ches. The pacifist Nasrid monarch then arrived at a rapid decision that has been
seen in very different lights by historians, depending on their particular outlook;
he decided to ally himself with Ferdinand in order to secure peace in his dominions.
This decision had a great influence on the development of the Granada we are
at pains to call authentic: that is to say, the Granada that unites two cultures and
two ways of life, blending them closely into an inseparable amalgam.

One historian has left an account of the scene that settled this decisive moment
of history: Banu 'l-Ahmar went secretly to the Christian encampment near Jaén
and presented himself before Ferdinand III with a humility not entirely devoid
of grandeur and said, " I am Mohammed, King of Granada. I have no wish
to be your enemy. I put my trust in your loyalty and place myself under your
protection. Take all that I possess and regard me as a vassal of Your Majesty. "
It seems that, on uttering these words which symbolized the political decline of
Islam, Banu 'l-Ahmar fell to his knees and kissed the Christian King's hands,
as a sign of his obeisance and submission. Apparently, Ferdinand was so moved
by this unexpected gesture that he determined not to appear less generous and
magnanimous than the man who, moments before, had been his enemy. He
raised him to his feet and embraced him cordially, made a pact with him and
refused the riches that were offered. He certainly admitted Banu 'l-Ahmar as
a vassal, but left him sovereignty within his domains on condition that he paid
an annual tribute. He also granted him the right to attend the Courts of Castile with the same status as a Christian noble, and reminded him of his new obligation to provide some fighting men for wars. This included wars against Moslems—it seems that there is no act of generosity that does not contain a certain
hidden cruelty.

From that moment, the Kingdom of Granada began to be a curious combination of Arab traditions and Christian innovations. Not only did outward customs
and fashions become Castilianized, but even the inner psychology of the people
of Granada underwent a gradual, but quite obvious change. The Arab historians
of the time regretted this loss of political and spiritual autonomy, without, of
course, being able to foresee that this fusion of the two cultures was thenceforth
to bring about the unique city that now holds our interest. " These Spanish
Arabs," says Ibn Khaldun, " have lost the spirit of co-operation and mutual aid,
the *asabiyya*, which produces political power. They only hold on to their family
trees... Because they are subdued by force and are tired of being humiliated, they
imagine that a good family background and a post in the government are all
that are necessary to conquer a kingdom and rule over other men."

Another historian, Ibn Said, also talks of the change in customs at that time
and says that, at the beginning of the Nasrid Dynasty, the Andalusians' dress
" was like that of their Christian neighbours and rivals: broad cuirasses, appended
shields, heavy helmets, broad-pointed lances, shapeless saddle-trees and banners
attached to the rear of the saddles. Each soldier bore a device to symbolize his
particular arms and an escutcheon by which he was recognized." This opinion
was fully shared by al-Khatib who assures us that " the turban is no longer worn
by Banu 'l-Ahmar, the ruler of the greatest part of al-Andalus. Both sultans
and soldiers tend to adopt the clothing of their Christian neighbours. They use
the same weapons and their cloaks, including the scarlet ones, are also the same.
Identical, too, are their banners, their saddles and their method of warfare with

shields and long lances. They are not acquainted with Arabic clubs or bows; instead they use the Christian bows for besieging towns and the princes use them also for fighting in the field."

After concluding his pact with Ferdinand III, Banu 'l-Ahmar was soon obliged to fulfil the clause that dealt with the provision of an army and had to lead his men alongside Ferdinand's army against, paradoxically, the Moslem kingdom of Seville. Indeed, his first engagement was at the siege of the city of Seville itself. Banu 'l-Ahmar left Granada with five hundred chosen warriors, of whom it has been said that they were extremely dexterous in horsemanship and lance-throwing. It was a sad and humiliating obligation, since they had to turn their weapons on members of their own faith—a demonstration of the hazards of political expediency. Nevertheless, Banu 'l-Ahmar achieved great fame for his deeds in that conquest and for having influenced Ferdinand to refrain from the harsher customs of war that were then prevalent. In 1248, Seville capitulated to the Castilian and Moslem besiegers and Mohammed Banu 'l-Ahmar was free to return heavy-hearted and taciturn to his domain, more regretful than proud of his triumphs. He now saw clearly the ever increasing threats to the cause of Islam and, it is said, would from time to time utter such exclamations as "How poor and wretched our lives would be if our hopes were not so high and great!"

When Banu 'l-Ahmar sadly entered his capital, his subjects, unlike some other Moslems, did not regard his behaviour as a betrayal of their faith and gave him an enthusiastic reception. Indeed, they saw him more as a benefactor than as a hero. Mankind has always sought after peace more than glory and Banu 'l-Ahmar was the creator of his people's happiness, therefore they could not stop to consider a few political lapses. They had erected triumphal arches for their Sultan and they unanimously acclaimed him al-Ghalib ("the Conqueror"). Some chroniclers tell us that when he heard this cry, Mohammed Banu 'l-Ahmar turned and exclaimed "Wa al-Ghalib bi 'llah" ("Only God is the Conqueror"). This saying was immortalized as the personal motto of the Nasrid monarch and was inscribed on his coat of arms along a traverse bar. It also survived as the motto of his descendants and it is to be seen at every turn in the Alhambra (ill. 47). Banu 'l-Ahmar had obtained peace and prosperity at the cost of submitting himself, however loosely, to the Christian yoke; but he knew that when certain heterogeneous elements are in conflict, separated by deep and indelible hostile impulses, harmony cannot be certain or permanent. Therefore, following the advice of an old maxim "Arm yourself in peace-time and wrap up well till summer-time", he used the respite he had gained to fortify his dominions and equip his arsenals, at the same time encouraging the useful arts that make nations rich and powerful. He awarded grants and privileges to the best craftsmen of the nation. He fostered the breeding of horses and other useful animals. He promoted agriculture and instigated improvements in the fertility of the land until the fine valleys of the kingdom blossomed like gardens. He also granted great privileges to the silk industry to ensure that the fabrics made in Granada would surpass those of Syrian manufacture in quality and beauty. Moreover, he promoted the mining of gold, silver and other metals discovered in the mountainous areas of his domains and he was the first king of Granada to have coins bearing his name minted in those metals, emphasizing that the moulds should be neatly inscribed.

It was about that time, towards the middle of the thirteenth century, soon after his victorious return from Seville, that the Sultan began work on the Alhambra. He himself inspected the operation, mingling with the architects and decorators and directing the work with extraordinary diligence. We must not forget that he was building a peaceful and handsome home for himself. Contemporary chroniclers and some later commentators tell us that Banu 'l-Ahmar was modest in his ways and behaviour. His pastimes were very restrained and his dress was unostentatious and hardly differed from that of his vassals. He had a harem, as had all Moslem monarchs, but in his there were not many concubines and these lived in magnificent style but were little visited by him. His wives were the daughters of the most illustrious noblemen of his Court, and he treated them as true companions and friends, not with the usual Arabic disdain. Even stranger, he managed to get these women to live together in peace and harmony.

Banu 'l-Ahmar would spend much of the day strolling deep in thought in the tranquil shade of his gardens. He read a great deal and had many books read to him. Amid the red walls of the Alhambra an ideal atmosphere of contemplation began to make itself felt. Despite this, the King did not overlook the education and welfare of his people. He also imposed a heavy programme of study on his three sons, who were taught by celebrated mentors sought out by their father. Mohammed Banu 'l-Ahmar never broke the promise he had given the Castilian King and when Ferdinand died in Seville in 1254, the Sultan sent his condolences to his son and successor, Alfonso X, who was to be known to history as Alfonso the Wise. On that mournful occasion, the Nasrid King sent a hundred Moslem horsemen, who kept watch over the saintly monarch's body, each bearing a large lighted taper. This ceremony was repeated every year around the dead King's tomb. This serves to indicate that Banu 'l-Ahmar's submission to Ferdinand was no mere flattery but was based on a sincere loyalty.

One day, when he was seventy-nine years of age, Banu 'l-Ahmar led out a party of handpicked warriors in order to suppress an *algara* or revolt that had broken out in one of his dominions. It happened that, as they were riding out of Granada, one of the chieftains noticed that their Sultan accidentally broke his lance against the lintel of the city gate. This event was regarded as an ill omen by the Court officials who begged him to abandon the enterprise and return to the Palace. Their pleas were useless and the Sultan rode on. The omen was soon fulfilled. According to the Arab chroniclers, at dusk on that day Banu 'l-Ahmar was suddenly stricken by a mysterious illness. He was about to fall from his horse when his attendants saved him and he was carried back to Granada on a palanquin. But before they reached the city he grew worse and it became necessary to place him in a tent that they pitched on the Vega. There the first Nasrid monarch spent his last moments in agonizing pain, accompanied by vomiting of blood and frightful spasms, in sight of the crimson towers of his Alcázar. The life of Mohammed Banu 'l-Ahmar was rich in positive actions and is full of significance for the later history of Granada. But the outstanding symbol of his reign was the inauguration of the Alhambra. It was he who really founded what the historians call Nasrid art.

Yusuf I was one of the most significant of his successors. A great deal has been written of him, perhaps not so much as he merits, though one Romantic writer spoke of him with great enthusiasm: Abu 'l-Hadjdjadj Yusuf acceded to the throne of Granada in the year 1333 and his personal endowments and intellectual accomplishments won him a general popularity that portended both a happy and prosperous reign. He was of noble bearing and was endowed with extraordinary physical strength and good looks. His skin was too pale however, and, according to Arab historians, he increased his grave and majestic appearance by growing a beard which he dyed very black. He had a fantastic memory which he exercised in matters of science and learning. He was considered one of the best poets of his day, but this was not extraordinary in Moslem monarchs at that time. His manner was extremely courteous and affable. Yusuf was courageous but he was more disposed to peace than to war and considered himself utterly thwarted when there was nothing for it but to take up arms, a situation common enough in those days. His good nature was evident even in battle, for he forbade any unnecessary act of cruelty and strove to keep the horrors of warfare from women and children, the aged and the sick, those bound by religious vows and all who led an exemplary and good life.

Among his least successful enterprises figures the campaign he waged against the Kings of Castile and Portugal, which ended with the memorable battle of the Salado where Yusuf suffered a disastrous defeat which inflicted the *coup de grâce* on the power of the Spanish Moslems. In the truce he obtained after this rout, Yusuf devoted himself to the education of his people and to the improvement of their way of life. He set up schools in every village, which followed simple and uniform educational methods. He made it compulsory for each village of more than twelve houses to have a mosque and he prohibited the various abuses that had been introduced into religious ceremonies and public festivals. Yusuf maintained strict public order, instituting night patrols, and personally supervised municipal affairs. He displayed great energy in finishing the buildings begun by his predecessors, he ordered other new buildings to be constructed, including the Puerta de la Justicia, and he undertook the ornamentation of many of the *patios* and halls of the Alhambra as is shown by the numerous inscriptions of his name on the walls of the palace. He also built the fine Alcázar in Málaga, now completely in ruins.

There is no doubt that in those days the character of the monarch was faithfully reflected outside the royal circle. The noblemen and magnates of Granada imitated Yusuf's refined taste and enriched the city with opulent palaces, the halls of which were decorated with mosaic floors, and walls and domes finely worked in stucco, skilfully painted in gold and bright colours, or elegantly inlaid with cedar and other precious woods; some of these palaces have survived in a reasonably good state of preservation. Most of them had fountains and waterspouts that cleansed and cooled the air, and small wooden towers covered with a metal lamina to deflect the scorching rays of the sun. The sophisticated taste and artistic refinements that existed at that moment in Granada's history were such that a Moslem historian wrote: "the Granada of Yusuf's reign was like a silver chalice encrusted with emeralds and jacinths". A simple anecdote will shed some light on Yusuf's character: the long truce that followed the Battle of the Salado was about to expire and all the King of Granada's efforts to have it extended were useless. His mortal enemy, the Castilian King Alfonso XI, led out his forces and besieged the fortress of Gibraltar. Very much against his will, Yusuf was obliged to gather an army to relieve the town. But in the middle of his reluctant preparations, news came that a sudden disease had killed his bitter foe, the King of Castile. Instead of indulging in justifiable rejoicing, the Nasrid monarch merely said sadly and generously: " The world has lost one of its greatets princes. He was a sovereign who recognized merit both in his friends and in his enemies ". All the Spanish chroniclers unanimously extolled this trait of nobility. They tell us, too, that the Moorish warriors shared their monarch's grief and went into mourning for Alfonso XI. Even the besieged men of Gibraltar laid down their arms when they heard the news. When the Christian forces, who now lacked a leader, abandoned the siege, all the frontier sheiks allowed the funeral *cortège* to pass on its way from Gibraltar to Seville.

Yusuf did not long survive the enemy he had so generously mourned. One day in 1354, when he was worshipping in the Royal Mosque in the Alhambra, a madman's dagger plunged into his side. He died some hours afterwards. The assassin was quartered and his remains were burned in public to appease the rage of the people.

While the Castilian armies were gradually whittling away the land held by the Nasrid Sultans, violent internal struggles broke out in that territory, which destroyed the unity of the remaining Spanish Moslems. Civil war was waged in Granada by the Sultan Abu 'l-Hasan, his brother al-Zaghall and his favourite Zoraya (a former Christian, whose real name was Isabel de Solís) on the one hand, and by Boabdil, the Sultan's son, and his mother Aisha on the other. Boabdil was taken prisoner by the Christians during an attack on the town of Lucena and he came to terms with King Ferdinand, who saw in this a way of aggravating the Moslems' internal strife. One by one, cities and fortresses continued to fall into Christian hands. Abu 'l-Hasan abdicated in favour of al-Zaghall, who became ruler of almost the whole of the Sultanate, while Boabdil was governor of a part of the city of Granada, not much more than the Alhambra itself. The Moslem political situation was thus rather complicated. Between 1486 and 1489, the Christians captured Loja, Vélez Málaga, Málaga, Baza, Almería and Guadix, and al-Zaghall finally surrendered, selling his few remaining lands to the Christians and going into exile in North Africa. In 1491, the Catholic Kings began to besiege the city of Granada in earnest and, a few miles away, set up a camp that they were later to make into the town of Santafé (" Holy Faith ")—a name symbolic of their attitude to the Reconquest, which they regarded as a holy crusade. The havoc wrought on the Vega, the knowledge that no reinforcements would ever arrive to relieve the besieged city, and the firm resolution of the Castilian Monarchs, made Boabdil decide to surrender, and, together with his household, he departed into exile.

The life and character of Boabdil, who was the last Moorish king in Spain, were particularly tragic. Not for nothing did his subjects call him *al-Zogoybi*, " the poor devil ". Moreover, he has often been calumniated in literature and legend. The source of the allegations about his failings and even his crimes is probably to be found, as his vigorous defender Washington Irving claimed, in Pérez de Hita's book entitled *The Civil Wars in Granada*. Some of the actions imputed to him can be ascribed more definitely to his father Abu 'l-Hasan. It seems that it was the latter who put to death the illustrious Abencerrages, because, according to some accounts, he suspected them of being involved in a conspiracy to depose him, but, according to others, because one of that tribe had fallen in love with his favourite wife, the beautiful Zoraya.

Irving asserts also that the story about the accusation made against Boabdil's mother and her imprisonment in a tower can be regarded as another of Abu 'l-Hasan's cruel acts. In his old age, this bloodthirsty Sultan had taken to wife the noble Christian captive, Isabel, who bore him two sons. This ambitious woman wanted her sons to inherit the throne. In order to further her aims, she poisoned the mind of the Sultan, who in any case was distrustful by nature, against the sons of his other wives and concubines, by accusing them of plotting to depose

Detail of stucco decoration in the Sala de las Dos Hermanas at the Alhambra.

and assassinate him. The Sultan at once ordered some of them to be executed. Aisha la Horra, the virtuous mother of Boabdil, had once been Abu 'l-Hasan's favourite, but she, too, became a target for his suspicions. He imprisoned her and her son in the Torre de Comares and such was his fury that he would have put Boabdil to death, had Aisha not arranged his escape: one night she knotted together her sash and those of her attendants and lowered him from the tower, whence he fled to Guadix.

Irving goes on to say that, in his brief and turbulent reign, Boabdil showed himself to possess a character that was kindly and even tender. He was always ready to be merciful and never imposed harsh sentences on those who were constantly rebelling against him. He was courageous in battle, but lacked strength of mind;

in moments of crisis he would flounder in a sea of perplexity and indecision. This mental failing hastened his downfall and robbed him of any heroism that would have permitted him to take a more dignified place in history. Among the paintings in the gallery of the Generalife Palace hangs Boabdil's portrait. In it his countenance is kindly, handsome and melancholy, his complexion rubicund and his hair blond. If it is a good likeness, he certainly could have been changeable and indecisive, but not at all cruel or bloodthirsty.

The place where legend has it that Boabdil was imprisoned by his father is a vaulted room in the Torre de Comares, under the Salón de los Embajadores. From there a narrow passage leads to a similar room, where his mother Aisha was incarcerated. The walls are extremely thick and the windows are secured with iron bars. A narrow stone gallery with a small parapet extends along two sides of the tower, under the windows, but at a considerable height from the ground. It may have been from here that Aisha, with the aid of her servants, lowered Boabdil to safety.

Many other strange tales are told of Boabdil. It is said that, when he left the Alhambra to surrender to the Catholic Kings, he begged them not to allow anyone to pass through that gate again. According to some contemporary accounts, Isabella favoured the granting of his request and the gate was walled up. It stood in the centre of the tower known as the Torre de los Siete Suelos (Tower of the Seven Storeys), which was to be considered haunted by later generations. This once impregnable tower was blown up by the French when they abandoned the fortress.

From one of the heights of the Alpujarra Range which is approached by the Cuesta de las Lágrimas (Slope of Tears), Boabdil turned to take his last look at Granada, on his way into exile. In that spot there is a rock on which he is popularly supposed to have sat at that heart-breaking moment; the place is now known as El Suspiro del Moro (The Moor's Sigh). Perhaps it was there that he heard his mother's famous reproach, " Weep like a woman for what you could not defend like a man ". It is said that when Bishop Guevara told Charles V of that reproach, the Emperor replied in equally contemptuous terms, " If I had been in his place and he in mine, I should sooner have made the Alhambra my tomb than live in the Alpujarra without a kingdom ".

The Christian Conquest

On the morning of the second of January 1492, the Catholic Kings made their solemn entry into the Alhambra. The silver cross and the purple banner of Castile had just been placed on the Torre de la Vela. On the threshold of the Alcazaba, the Governor Yusuf ben Comija had handed over the keys to Ferdinand and Isabella. They, however, did not spare a glance for the fine palaces and scenery that surrounded them. They perhaps felt a little uneasy as they entered the last stronghold of those who had ruled over more than half the Peninsula for a very long period. In any case, Ferdinand and Isabella must have had many grave worries at that moment. They entrusted the keys of the fortress to the Count of Tendilla, whom they appointed Captain General of the Kingdom of Granada and Governor of the Alhambra. They garrisoned the walls and towers with their infantry and, after receiving a delegation of Moorish notables, they spent their first night in the palace, above the silent and apparently deserted city.

The Moorish surrender, in fact, solved none of their problems. It is a mistake to think that the capture of Granada marked the end of Spanish Islam and that

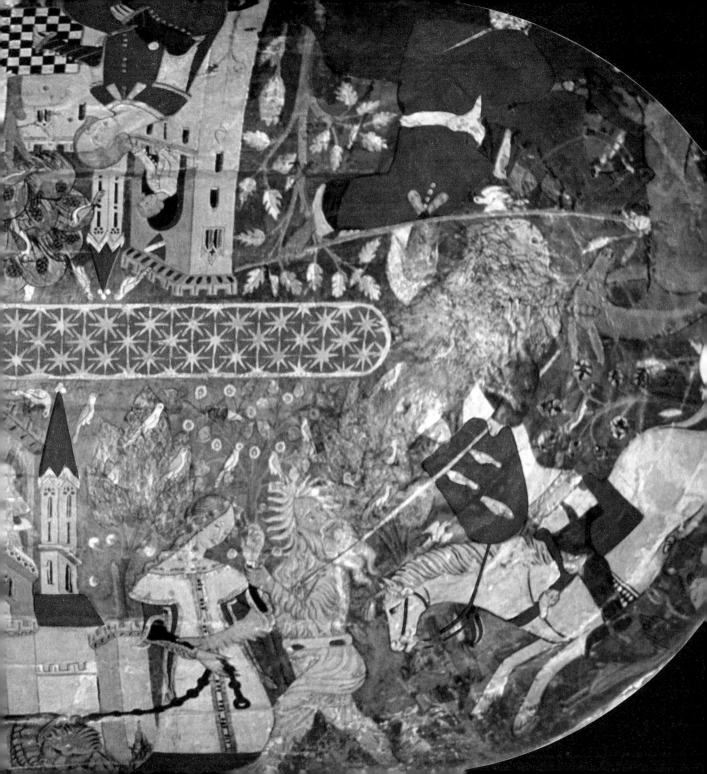

afterwards there were, on the one hand, Moslem subjects loyal to the Catholic Kings and, on the other, fanatical Christians relentlessly persecuting those Moslems. The truth is that there continued to exist in Spain an alien people who had once been victorious but were now vanquished, and who were quietly awaiting their punishment. This was predicted by their soothsayers, who had also foretold their defeat. Moreover, this race was not confined to the Kingdom of Granada, but was scattered throughout the Peninsula and maintained dangerous contacts with North Africa.

No one outside Spain could understand why the Christian Conquest had been so slow, and even less why, once the Spaniards had won back their territory, they did not get rid of the Moors, either by extermination or by expulsion. Earlier, in the thirteenth century, when the Almohad invasion was at its most threatening, the contingents who had been sent from beyond the Pyrenees to help the Castilian forces were indignant at the consideration shown to the captured Moors. After the battle of Las Navas de Tolosa, the French Archbishop of Narbonne, who fought with the Christian forces, openly criticized the terms that the Castilians made with the inhabitants of Úbeda, which allowed them to retain not only their goods but also their town and the surrounding lands. The Archbishop considered that the agreement flouted God himself and constituted a veritable sacrilege. Many years later, when Francis I of France was being held prisoner in Madrid by Charles V, the history of Granada was read to him and he is said to have exclaimed, "What about the Moors? Haven't they been expelled? Well, then, everything is as before!"

Indeed, nearly everything was as before; but neither the French nor any other foreigners were able to grasp the motives of expediency that led the Spaniards to act in the way they did. When the Kings of Castile and Aragon allowed the Moors to remain on Spanish soil and granted them virtual self-government in Christian territory, they were striving to avoid the depopulation of the reconquered areas; they had no wish to ruin the trade and agriculture of their new domains. Furthermore, it was the custom of Spanish Christian princes to establish protectorates that paid tributes to them rather than to achieve absolute rule by expulsion or extermination. The truth is that the whole of Christian Spain had lived for centuries off the taxes paid by the Moors.

From all this it can be inferred that the Spaniards had only reconquered these lands on paper. A sheaf of parchment documents, covered with signatures and affixed with lead seals hanging from silk ribbons, acknowledged the Christian monarchs as owners of the various castles and towns that had been surrendered. They had conquered as much by astute diplomacy as by force of arms. Nevertheless, the hardest task remained unaccomplished: the task either of assimilating the vanquished, or of eliminating them. Basically, such an assimilation was fraught with difficulties, especially in the religious sphere. On the other hand, after eight centuries of co-existence and intermarriage, the Moors and Christians had grown very like one another in behaviour, customs and even character, to such an extent that an unconscious interchange of cultures had taken place. While many Arabs had long been Castilianized, numerous Castilians were becoming practically Arabized. Purists on both sides expressed their disapproval of these changes.

The conditions of the capitulation of Granada contain no less than fifty-five articles and are a document of great historical interest. The Catholic Kings' main aim was to convince the people of Granada that the surrender would be to their

49. Arches in the Patio de los Arrayanes, decorated in stucco with characteristic floral, geometric and stalactite motifs, and inscriptions in praise of the Sultan and Allah.

advantage, because they would become subjects of more humane rulers than the Nasrid Sultans. Instead of being ruled by tyrants who imposed oppressive taxes on them yet failed to defend them, they would be loyal vassals of powerful monarchs who would treat them with kindness and moderation. This was a special point in the treaty, emphasized by both parties: " The governors and justices that Their Majesties may from time to time appoint to rule the city, the Albaicín and the other lands concerned in this capitulation, must act in such a manner as to honour the vanquished and fulfil all the terms of this treaty. "

In addition, the treaty forbade Christians from entering the mosques without the permission of the *alfaquíes*; neither were they to enter Moorish dwellings, nor hold dances and feastings if their neighbours objected. Moreover, on the day the Spaniards were to enter the Alhambra, the Christian troops were not to march through the city; they would go around the city walls, in order not to provoke incidents. The Spanish soldiers were not to climb on to the walls separating the Alcazaba from the Albaicín, because from there they might see things they should not in the houses of the Moorish quarter. The victors could not have shown more consideration for the customs and susceptibilities of the conquered.

Absolute liberty of conscience and freedom of worship were proclaimed. The Moslems retained their mosques, minarets and muezzins. Conversions to Christianity had to be voluntary. " If any dispute arises among the aforesaid Moors, " says the treaty, " they shall be judged by their own law and custom ." They were also allowed to keep their property, both real and personal. As for taxes, it was agreed " that the said Moors shall not have to pay Their Majesties more dues than those they were wont to pay the Moorish kings ".

Another important point was that the Moors were not obliged to do military service. Furthermore, if they did not wish to become subjects of the new monarchs, they could cross to Africa in ships provided by Their Majesties with their personal safety guaranteed. They would be allowed to go to Barbary or Morocco with all their goods and merchandise, including gold, silver, jewels, arms and horses. If Africa did not suit them, they were granted the right to return to the Kingdom of Granada within three years and once more enjoy the protection of the terms of the capitulation. Merchants would be permitted to come and go in complete safety throughout all the lands and dominions of the Catholic Kings, and even to cross to Africa, without paying any more customs dues than those paid by Christians. All these details are finally confirmed by one general formula in the treaty: the people of Granada " shall be honoured, favoured and well treated as servants and vassals by Their Majesties and by their representatives ".

Both sides accepted this form of co-existence and appear to have kept their distance for many years. Nevertheless, a number of Christians married Moorish women; indeed, many Moorish women wanted nothing better than to make such a match. Marriages between Moors and Christian women were also not uncommon. In the artistic sphere, too, the contacts between the two cultures, which had been maintained for many centuries, were now greatly increased. Moorish art had spread into much of Christian Spain and even over the Pyrenees during the thirteenth, fourteenth and fifteenth centuries. It influenced the Gothic style, but itself took on Gothic elements. With the introduction of the Mudejar style, the decoration of Spanish architecture became more elaborate and complex. The door of Salamanca Cathedral, for example, illustrates clearly how the Spanish sculptors imitated the Moorish arabesques by working marble in the same way as the Moslems worked plaster, leaving no part of the surface unadorned. The same influence is even more obvious in the Diputación of Barcelona, especially in the sculpted ornamentation of the door of the Capilla de San Jorge; although the general outline is Gothic, there is a definite imitation of the Mudejar style.

Arabic influence is most notable in poetic forms of the period. The short ballads of the Romancero recall the poetry of the Andalusian Moslems by their themes, which are generally historical and military, or erotic and courtly. It is not improbable that the refinements of gongorism were an echo of the rhetorical tricks of the earlier Arabic poets; not to mention the Andalusian songs of today, with the ghosts of al-Mutamid and Ibn Ammar pervading the *saetas* and the *seguidillas*.

Spaniards and Europeans in general were especially indebted to the Peninsular Arabs for the scholastic philosophy taught in the universities of Cordoba, Seville and Saragossa, an Arabized form of Graeco-Roman Scholasticism, which soon spread elsewhere. In addition, their schools were well versed in medicine, mathematics, astronomy, and above all astrology, alchemy and demonology—this last occult branch of learning attracted students from the whole of Christian Europe in the Middle Ages. Europe's greatest gain from Moslem Spain, however, was the philosophy of Aristotle, sifted and brought up to date by Averroes, the Cordoban Moslem philosopher.

Life and Art under the Nasrids
Under the Nasrid monarchs, the city of Granada lay at the foot of the hills on which the unique Alcázar of the Alhambra stood, and then consisted of a complex network of suburbs, typical now of Moroccan towns and earlier of European medieval cities. One of the oldest and most important quarters is the Albaicín, built on a steep hillside that rises abruptly above the stony bed of a torrent and forms a rocky gorge with the hill nearest to the Alhambra. This quarter was the real core of the Moslem city and later of the Morisco city. As we have already noted, the first sovereigns of Granada had built a strong fortress, called the Alcazaba Cadima (Old Fort) to distinguish it from the Alcazaba Chedib (New Fort), and the Albaicín quarter proper, which occupied the highest point among those hills, except for Sabika itself. On the gentler slopes that descend to the Vega stood the less ancient quarters of the Zenete, Bibarrambla and Antequeruela. As for the Alhambra, or rather, the site it occupies, it was a fortified spot from the ninth century onwards, but it did not come into its full grandeur until the Nasrid epoch, that is to say, from the end of the thirteenth century to the end of the fourteenth, omitting the years of decline in the fifteenth century.

Like all Arabic cities, Granada is not monumental. "The houses of this city", said Mármol, a sixteenth-century chronicler of Granada, "were built so close together in Moorish times and the streets were so narrow that there was no more than an arm's breadth between the windows across the street and there were many quarters where horsemen carrying lances could not penetrate." The main public buildings were mosques, which were numerous and in the main constructed before the Nasrid period, schools and hospitals. Mármol adds that the structures were African in style. It would be more accurate, however, to state that the African houses were built in Spanish style, since the Berbers and other peoples of the Maghrib merely imitated the work of their Andalusian Mohammedan brothers whom they considered to be the founders of the nation's heritage of art and literature.

Many of these original public buildings disappeared or were rebuilt as time went on. The *suks* or markets, on the other hand, because they were in constant use, were better preserved. As in all Berber towns, these markets were surrounded by high walls with heavy gates studded with bolts and iron fittings. One of these was called the Alcaicería or Silk Market, of which traces still remain. It was made up of tiny shops or stalls, similar to those in the Roman markets (out of which, to some extent, the Berber markets may be said to have developed), situated in a confusing maze of narrow passages that were often roofed, where the merchants assembled in guilds, according to the nature of their trade. There they proffered the type of merchandise that can still be seen in similar establishments in Africa and the Middle East; but there were also specialities of Granada, above all wrought gold bracelets, bangles, ear-rings and other trinkets, and the famous gold brocades. It appears that women at that time had a great love of elegance and luxury, and bought all kinds of expensive cloths, ostentatious fabrics, trinkets and ornaments. They wore elegantly made slippers, similar to those now worn by women in the interior of Algeria; and naturally they hid their faces behind the traditional veil—a custom that still persisted only a few years ago in some villages of definite Morisco origin in the South of Spain, such as Mojácar, Vejer de la Frontera and Tarifa.

The *suks* of Granada were in their way important commercial centres and provided the funds for public finance. Of course, the vital part of the economy of the kingdom, and in particular of the city of the Nasrids, was the agricultural produce. The Vega was extremely well cultivated at that time and was covered with gardens and orchards, water-mills and windmills, farmhouses and tiny villages, ranches and country retreats. These leafy, shaded spots, like rich oases, abundant with all kinds of plants and fruit-trees and well provided with water, lying in the middle of a territory that is for the most part scorched and arid, have throughout history imbued the onlooker with a sense of wonderment. The wealth of this tiny kingdom, which was the most fertile and best cultivated in the whole of Spain, lay in agriculture. The rich Vega of Granada was always a source of amazement for foreigners. In the time of Charles V, the Venetian Ambassador, Andrea Navaggiero, was stunned by the sight of such abundance. The figs grown in Granada, like those of Málaga, were famous throughout the Mediterranean; they were exported not only to Egypt and Syria, but also, according to al-Makkari, to India and China. The Kingdom of Granada also produced a type of wheat that was much sought after. Nowhere else was there such fine bread—a bread that was close-grained and very white (this bread is still baked in Spain), the recipe for which was taken to Africa by Moorish exiles.

Ibn al-Khatib, the last great literary figure of Moslem Spain, has left us a description of Granada under the Nasrid Dynasty. This chronicler wrote a work entitled *The Full Moon Splendour of the Nasrid Dynasty*, which contains a true history of the Kingdom of Granada and its institutions and customs, its kings and its riches. We include here a page or two of this work, because of its documentary value:

" The strangely named city of Granada, the Spanish Damascus, is a city in the Elvira region; the town of Elvira itself had flourished previously on a site four miles away. Granada became a court in the fourth century of the Hegira and rapidly increased in greatness and power. The city is today the metropolis of the coastal towns, the illustrious capital of the whole kingdom, a great marketplace for traders, a pleasing hostess to travellers of all nations, a perpetual garden of flowers, a splendid orchard of fruit-trees, an enchantment for all living creatures, the centre of public finance, a place famous for its fields and forts, a vast

50. Small fountain at one end
of the pool in the Patio de los
Arrayanes at the Alhambra.

sea of wheat and fine vegetables and an inexhaustible source of silk and sugar. Nearby soar lofty peaks, notable for the whiteness of their snow and the excellence of their water. Moreover, Granada enjoys health-giving breezes, many beguiling gardens and several exquisite herbs and perfumes: its most singular merit being that all the year round there are cornfields and pleasant green meadows. The area abounds in gold, iron, silver, lead, pearls and sapphires, and its woods are full of blue gentian and lavender. Lastly, there is produced cochineal and enough silk to supply the home market easily, as well as outside trading. There is not a shadow of doubt that the clothes made of this silk surpass the silks of Syria in softness, delicacy and lasting quality...

" The natural setting is most pleasing and rivals the valley of Damascus; one can journey through it with equal ease on foot or on horseback, by day or by night. Nature has bestowed all her luxuriance on this plain and has refreshed it with delightful springs. It is dotted with pleasant villages, mansions and gardens, and beautified by dense and handsome groves; a line of hills and mountains looms on the horizon and encloses an area of many square miles within a wide semi-circle. The great city of Granada with its suburbs lies partly on the hills and partly on the plain. It is not easy to describe the comfort and beauty provided there by the mildness of the winds and breezes, the solidity of the bridges, the magnificence of its temples and the breadth of its squares. The famous River Darro rises at its eastern confines and flows through the town, dividing its suburbs, then changes course and meets the River Genil, which, after lapping the city walls, flows on through the spacious plain, now swollen by other torrents and streams, and finally directs its proud course, Nile-like, towards Seville...

" The regal residence of the Alhambra presents a fine appearance, rising like a second city. The enclosure is embellished with lofty towers, thick walls, sumptuous halls and other elegant buildings. Sparkling torrents rush downwards, soon becoming quiet brooks that murmur through the shady woods. Just like the city below, the Alhambra has so many orchards and gardens that the palace turrets are glimpsed amid a canopy of foliage, like bright stars in the night sky. All around, the vines wreathe trees laden with apples and other delightful fruit. The nearby gardens produce so many vegetables and cereals that only a prince with his great treasure could pay a fair price for them. The annual rent of each garden amounts to fifty *áureos*, as well as a tribute of thirty pounds to the sovereign. The incessant crop-bearing quality of this land results in perpetual tillage and its produce in our day would be estimated at twenty-five thousand *áureos*. The king possesses luxurious leisure rooms made delightful by the woods and the infinite variety of plants...

" Wherever one looks, one sees handsome towers. The streams flow in different directions, sometimes to supply the baths, sometimes to work the water-mills, the income from which is earmarked for the restoration of the city walls. These properties extend for some miles and many honest farmers and hard-working animals are employed in tilling them. Almost everywhere castles and sacred temples are being constructed. The fertile nature of the soil facilitates and encourages the labour of it. On the estates many pleasant villages are built and the plain is so wide that there is always a rich crop and ample provision for grazing, common land, watering places and ranches. There are about three hundred villages and a hundred and thirty water-mills in the immediate vicinity of Granada and fifty colleges and temples within the city."

Al-Khatib does not content himself merely with this geographical description

51. One of the doors in the Patio de los Arrayanes.

of Granada in his day, which might well serve also for the modern city; he goes on to give us valuable information about the customs of its inhabitants during the Nasrid period:

" The people of Granada are orthodox in religious matters; there are some members of the Malakid Sect, but this heresy has not infected their spirit. They are loyal to their kings and extremely patient and generous; they are generally slim, of medium height and well proportioned, with black hair. They speak an elegant form of Arabic, and their speech is full of proverbs and occasionally rather too abstract. In discussion they tend to be unyielding and hot-headed. Like the Persians, they dress in fine clothes of silk, wool and cotton, striped in subtle shades. In winter they wrap themselves in the African cloak or the Tunisian burnous. In summer they wear white linen. The faithful assembled in the temple arrayed in their many-hued clothing present the appearance of a spring meadow covered in flowers...

" The army is divided into two classes: the warriors of Granada and the recruits from Africa. The soldiers of Granada will take orders only from a prince of the Dynasty or a high dignitary of State. In earlier times they used cuirasses, broad breast-plates, shields, vizors and other defensive armour, and as offensive weapons they had long lances with double points, scimitars and spears. Each squadron or company had an *alférez* or ensign who bore a standard. Slowly improvements have taken place in military discipline and in the quality of the arms; they have adopted smaller cuirasses, light helmets, saddles of the *jineta* type with short stirrups, leather shields and sharper lances... The African cohorts are made up of various peoples. They are divided into groups in the command of their own captains who come under the authority of a superior officer, normally a noble and close relative of the kings of Fez. Very few of them wear the Persian turban, thus following the example of the people of Granada, of whom only the priests, magistrates and doctors continue wearing it. Their favourite weapon is a spear with several blades, which they hurl at their enemy with amazing dexterity. They live in poorly built barracks and on feast days they dress elegantly and frequent the hostelries, setting a pernicious example for young people with their noisy merry-making and their bawdy songs...

" Part of the diet of the people of Granada is wheaten bread; the poor families and the labourers eat barley bread in the hard days of winter. The markets are full of every kind of fruit, especially the grapes harvested on the fertile fields of Granada. These are so plentiful that the income from them is calculated nowadays at fourteen thousand *áureos*. The country is well stocked with other fruits, such as figs, raisins, apples, pomegranates, chestnuts, acorns, hazelnuts and almonds, all of which are to be found throughout the year. Moreover, some grapes are preserved for out of season use... The coinage of Granada, made of pure gold and silver, is characterized by its exquisite minting. Those citizens dedicated to their tasks stay aloof from the bustle of the court, especially at harvest times, and spend the summer at their pleasant farms. Others, instilled with a warlike spirit, live on the frontiers to harry the Christians with their bold raids and to act as a defence for their fellow citizens. Among the ornaments thought particularly tasteful by the princesses and ladies of Granada are girdles, sashes, garters and coifs, exquisitely worked in faceted gold and silver. Precious stones such as zircons, topazes and emeralds glisten amid their finery. The women of Granada are graceful, elegant and *svelte;* it is rare to find one who is ill proportioned. They are neat, take great pains to arrange their long hair and delight in displaying

their ivory-like teeth. The breath from their lips is as sweet as the perfume of
a flower. Their charms are highlighted by their graceful manners, exquisite
discretion and delightful conversation. It is regrettable, however, that we are
reaching a moment in which the women of Granada are carrying the magnificence
of their attire and adornment to the brink of fantasy."

From the mass of hyperbole that characterized the florid Moslem style,
emerges a detailed description of many aspects of the daily life and customs of
the people of Granada during the Nasrid period, which saw the opulent reign of
Mohammed Banu 'l-Ahmar and his successors.

The art of the Nasrid Dynasty is civic and courtly rather than military or
religious. Hardly any mosques or fortresses figure among its achievements.
Unlike the Almohads and the Umayyad Caliphs, the monarchs of the Banu
Nasr lineage had little use for temples or forts. One can say that Nasrid art
is a continuation of the traditional Islamic art of the Peninsula, enriched by Almohad elements and Oriental influences. But despite all these influences it possesses special characteristics that are markedly national in tone, such as the use
of the small, compact adornment. It was an art which followed Berber designs
and which was full of subtlety and the usually minute decorative refinement
found in all decadent artistic expression. It can be said that the construction of
the Patio de los Leones in Granada was the last achievement of Moslem art in
the Iberian Peninsula.

As well as minute decoration, the Nasrid architects could also create vast
buildings with strong, bare lines, such as the Tower of Comares and the Puerta
de la Justicia. The interiors of their buildings are skilfully designed; an example
is provided by the interior of the Casa Real as one climbs from the Patio
de los Leones to the Mirador de Daraja. In the city streets, this art created buildings as near perfect from the aesthetic point of view as from the functional. The
main materials used in them were glazed ceramics for the floor, plinths and façades;
neatly carved wood and chiselled plaster for the ceilings, fashioned into
mocárabes or stalactites, and filigrees; marble for the fountains and the paving of
the courtyards. Perhaps the most original and unusual aspect of this style is
the great quantity of columns used—columns topped by capitals with new
and distinct shapes, which are to be found both in the royal residences and in
the poorest dwellings.

The builders of Granada also possessed a unique ability that has rarely been
surpassed, of closely harmonizing their architecture with the natural surroundings, complementing both with fountains, sprays, streams and water-courses.
As we have already noted, the abstract character of their art caused them to
avoid almost any representation of living creatures. This resulted in a tendency
to what has since then been called arabesque, as well as to the use of gardens.
As we said earlier, there are only rare traces of Nasrid religious monuments.
Rather than exhibiting an ultramundane preoccupation, their constructions show
an inclination towards intelligent hedonism: they sought after a pleasant and
comfortable enjoyment of life, allied to serene contemplation of nature. As
one historian has remarked, the halls and dwellings of the Nasrids constitute
one of the most perfect and exquisite creations for the quiet enjoyment of human
existence within controlled natural surroundings. The materials of the fabric
were brittle, but they were handled with extraordinary skill and good taste.

The art historian Torres Balbás reminds us that Ibn Khaldun attributed the
fragile structure of the buildings of the Arabs to their earlier nomadic existence

and also to their great indifference to an art form as such. They have frequently been reproached for the poverty of their interior structure and the fragility of their decorative roofing. But they were not constructing monuments for posterity; on the contrary, they were building pleasant but fragile homes to live in. " The walls of adobe and brick were covered in ceramics and painted plaster work; the beams and ceilings of badly fitted light wood were hidden behind artificial domes made of stucco *mocárabe* decorations or carved and painted woodwork. Above the marble columns in the alcoves, balconies, windows and porticos, brick pillars were built to support ill-fitting planks and wooden lintels which were hidden by moulded plaster plaques and arches placed between the lintels and the columns. In the same way, all the gaps were disguised with false arches." " Palaces constructed with a handful of sticks," Prieto Vives has commented. " Poor materials magically converted into an artistic fabric," says Gómez Moreno.

The architecture of Granada exhibits a disregard for the exterior appearance of the buildings, an outlook no doubt inherited from Byzantium. Very occasionally, doorways have some adornment. The doors of the dwellings are always interior, inside courtyards, even in the royal palaces. The external walls of the houses and palaces present a bare appearance, broken only by an occasional window high in the wall or a jutting wooden balcony with its lattice or coupled arched window. If the building is in the country, or set apart from other buildings, the upper floor has a series of windows with coupled arches or balconies.

" A Gothic cathedral," says Torres Balbás, " like a monastery or a medieval palace, is a complex architectural mass, built according to a preconceived plan. The architects of Granada did not create any architectural unit more complex than the *patio* or courtyard, with its surrounding arcades and its passage-ways to the façades... Not knowing how to arrange large unified blocks in which the components would remain harmonically integrated, when the programme was more vast than the *patio* unit would allow, they placed a number of *patios* alongside one another, as can clearly be seen in the Alhambra and elsewhere in Granada, in the Alcazaba of Málaga and even in a great Mudejar building like the Casa del Chapiz in Granada. The fragmentary lay-out of Moslem buildings encouraged this method." The Alhambra today, without its original doors, windows and lattices, gives the false impression of a reasonably good continuity of space. There existed and still exist balconies from which one can enjoy views of distant horizons, but the main halls were closed in, receiving only the light that entered through the small windows over the doors, the balconies that were generally latticed, and the openings situated high in the walls.

At the same time as this legendary palace was being built, the city of Granada was enriched by a series of important public buildings: the Alhóndiga Nueva, the Madraza and the Maristán. These three buildings conformed to a plan unprecedented in the Peninsula, imported from the Orient by way of Morocco. They all had the same lay-out: a central *patio* with surrounding open galleries that had adjoining halls. Because these were functional buildings, the brick pillars that support the galleries were left undecorated. But if the lay-out of these buildings was imported, the adaptation of the shapes and the careful detail are entirely local. In the public baths, which had a long tradition in Andalusian architecture, the earlier plan was followed with only slight innovations.

The decoration that is nearly always absent in military structures is to be found on the portals of the civic buildings, on and near the *mihrabs* in the mosques and above all inside the houses of the wealthy and in the palaces. Although the design of the structure and the shape of its various rooms might be independent, in decoration the direct Spanish Moslem tradition was followed and the walls were covered, as though they were tapestries, with an inexhaustible luxuriance. Châteaubriand thought that the arabesqued walls of the Alhambra presented the appearance of Oriental fabrics embroidered in the harem by a bored slave-girl. It is a flat, compact decoration, without blank spaces or contrasts, which almost totally blots out the background and lacks any sense of depth or perspective, and in which the colours (many of them now restored) play the leading part.

Ruined Moorish mill and Roman bridge over the Guadalquivir, Cordoba.

" The composition of the decoration was arranged by dividing the walls into rectangles which were in effect plaster tapestries, edged with inscribed borders. The vertical panels are divided by closed geometric figures, filled with small, infinitely repeating patterns that meet the surrounding polygonal frame." In conformity with this synthesis of the characteristics of Nasrid art made by Torres Balbás, we shall indicate its three outstanding decorative features: 1) the abundance of Kufic inscriptions; 2) the *attawriq* plaster work that almost always represents foliage in the abstract; 3) the interlacing geometric designs. On the basis of these three motifs, the Nasrids produced an intellectual and abstract art that was really, with its unique arabesques, an ingenious game. It was an art that consisted, as the same historian has said, of " sheer decorative rhetoric, more to be admired for the ingenuity of the detail than for the composition of the whole."

139

Entrance to the Torre de las dos Hermanas in the Alhambra. Engraving by F. Giomignani from a drawing by
Henry Swinburne; 1775.

Nevertheless, it is not the minutiae of the Nasrid art of Granada, although
they are on a grand scale, that really thrill the onlooker, but rather its atmosphere, the subtlety of its refinement, the approach to life that it suggests, or,
to put it another way, its human significance.

FROM THE ALBAICÍN
TO THE SACROMONTE

The Albaicín, the Alcazaba Cadima and the Alhambra lie on the sides of the Darro gorge. In spite of their many chapels and hermitages, they are still Moorish at heart: the twisting streets, the white buildings, the empty squares adorned by invading plants from the adjoining gardens, all combine to evoke a Moorish atmosphere. It was here that Granada first began in the dim past. The earliest settlers do not appear to have grasped the defensive value of this gorge: the first signs of human occupation are to be found on the plain, at the megalithic temple of Dilar and the ancient Christian necropolis of Gabia la Grande. The actual site of the ancient city of Illiberis, in 306 A.D. the scene of the famous Church Council, still poses a problem. Two theories have emerged from the heated archaeological disputes: the first claims that the city stood on the Sierra Elvira, which is named after Illiberis; the second favours Granada as the site, since Roman remains have been dug up in the Alcazaba Cadima. So far, the problem has not been solved; and since Illiberis probably meant " new city " in the Basco-Iberian tongue, another difficulty arises: was there an even older town, and if so, where was it situated?

During the twelfth and thirteenth centuries, Granada broke from the bounds of the red walls of the Alhambra and spread itself over the neighbouring hills. The last remaining Christian church, on the Paseo del Triunfo, had been destroyed in 1099, and Granada became even more Moorish. The constant pressure of the Castilian forces produced large numbers of refugees who took shelter in the Nasrid State. When Prince Ferdinand captured Baeza in 1227, the fugitives from that city settled on the hill where the Alcazaba Cadima stood, and they called it Baezín (" little Baeza "), that is to say, Albaicín. More fugitives poured into Granada during the campaigns of the fifteenth century: in 1410, the refugees from the city of Antequera established themselves outside Granada, in the quarter known as the Antequeruela (" little Antequera "), situated beneath the Ghetto.

Thus, the hills around Granada gradually became inhabited and the city itself expanded, until, when Boabdil surrendered in 1492, it had a population of almost 200,000 inhabitants, more or less the same as today. The new suburbs, which sprang up like mushrooms on the surrounding slopes, reached their heyday in the fourteenth and fifteenth centuries, as did the city itself. In that period the various quarters of Granada seemed to vie with one another in the manufacture of luxurious objects for the brilliant Nasrid Court. This was the epoch in which the marvellous minor arts and crafts flourished   The fine products of the repoussé-leather workers, the goldsmiths, the armourers, the filigreed-ivory craftsmen, the carpenters, the weavers and the makers of majolica ware—one of whose achievements was the famous vase (*ill.* 63) so admired by Théophile Gautier, which is now in the Alhambra Museum; all these products emerged from a host of workshops scattered throughout the city and were taken to the Court, or to the export merchants, or to the *suks*, such as the Alcaicería.

The Minor Arts

In the splendid Court of the Nasrids and among their subjects there were very close connections between commerce and art.   Spices, as well as skilled slaves, were imported from the Near East, and cereals and seasonings from North Africa.   The main markets for Granada's exports were in Africa and Christian Spain, where not only olive oil and fruit, but also and especially *objets d'art*, weapons, fabrics and the like were sold.   Baron de Davillier, one of the best researchers into the minor commercial arts of Spain, said that the Spaniards lived like country shepherds, unaware of their own wealth.   Even if this statement is no longer true, it was perfectly valid for the centuries before the Romantics discovered Spain.   No one, for instance, realized the value of the treasures that emerged from the workshops of Granada; they were appreciated only if they were made of gold or other precious materials.   *A propos* of this, Torres Balbás tells how Fortuny the painter, in the middle of the last century, came by the magnificent gilt porcelain vase which supported the holy water stoup in the church of Salar, probably for a mere handful of *pesetas*; he obtained another in an inn in the Albaicín quarter, where it was being used for storing water; and, in a house in the same suburb, he bought the famous Albaicín tile.   "A short time ago," says Torres Balbás, "we ourselves purchased for the Alhambra Museum, for quite a small sum, the doors of a closet, which are a perfect example of marquetry."

The Nasrid Sultanate possessed a growing body of craftsmen, who from the tenth century had worked throughout al-Andalus.   Their products were extraordinary: "all kinds of fabrics, especially sarsenets, fine silks with brightly coloured selvages; gold and silver embroidery; woollen carpets; ceramics of all sorts, from the commonest household utensils to huge gilt porcelain vases, now the pride of the museums and collections lucky enough to possess them; enamelled crystal, whose exquisite fragility accounts for the fact that hardly any unbroken examples have survived; beautiful ivory caskets, well worthy of their frequent use as urns for holy relics in Spanish churches; magnificent examples of marquetry, inlaid with unsurpassed skill and patience; swords and daggers with hilts wrought by outstandingly skilful goldsmiths; jewellery and many other products that, because of their great worth and fragility, have disappeared almost without trace."

One must become acquainted with the lesser ornamental crafts practised by the Moslem artists of Granada in the Nasrid period to have some idea of the exquisite and ingenious abilities of men's minds and hands when they are at their height.   Of all the fine crafts that once existed in Granada, the most notable was weaving and clothmaking, especially in silk.   Mulberry trees were planted everywhere, and the Alcaicería, or silk market, was famed the world over.   The Castilian chronicles of the Reconquest frequently mention the profusion and richness of the fabrics that originated in the Granada workshops.   One chronicle, which tells of the visit to Málaga (then a dependency of Granada) of Ad-

52. Detail of the stucco on the walls of the Patio de los Leones, with poetic and religious inscriptions, stylized foliage motifs and foiled arch.

miral Pero Niño and the Castilian galleys in 1404, gives a particularly detailed
account of Moorish fabrics. Following the Moslem custom of welcoming
guests, the Moors of Málaga took out to the galleys their *adaifas*, or presents,
which were so numerous that they were transported in small boats " refurbished
with drapings of silk and gold ". Some years later, in 1482, when the Marquis
of Cadiz captured Alhama—a deed immortalized in the famous and melancholy
frontier ballad " Ay de mi Alhama " (" Alas for my Alhama! ")—the Castilians'
rich booty included an abundance of " clothes of sarsenet and taffeta—thin woven
silk fabrics—and many other garments made of fine cloths ".

We have already noted al-Khatib's strictures on the excessive opulence in dress
of the ladies of Granada at one period of Nasrid rule, when they " bordered on
fantasy ". These ladies then wore magnificent girdles and sashes, garters and
coifs, made of finely wrought gold and silver. All the Moorish women in Granada wore embroidered collars, and the most elegant or wealthy had collars
embroidered in gold. That precious metal was also to be seen in the facings of
their voluminous white cloaks.

In Christian Spain during the Nasrid period, Moorish fabrics were held in
great esteem. The kings and nobles were interred in coffins lined with materials,
manufactured in Granada. Moreover, in life their clothes were made of fabrics
from the same source, which were also used for chasubles and for wrapping holy
relics. In the Nasrid Court there were silk weavers who produced multi-coloured
hoods and veils for the Moorish women, as well as materials for curtains and
screens. Some of the fabrics woven in Granada followed the style of the famous
brocades of Baghdad, patterned with bands bearing representations of animals
(the weavers having soon lost their distaste for images of living beings). In addition, the designs included geometric figures, interlacings of straight lines and curves,
polygonal stars, medallions etc. These motifs were placed on parallel bands,
in the same way as the decorative lettering, for which the cursive form was particularly popular. These designs are very similar to those used on the ceiling and
wall mouldings in the Alhambra; the same brilliant colours were used: golden
yellow, red, blue, black, green and white.

The crafts of embroidery and lace-making were directly related to the fabric
industry of Granada. Some of the silks produced were afterwards embroidered
like tapestries. Another common type of embroidery was of gold or silver thread
on leather, usually with *attawriq* ornamentation. The leather sheath of Boabdil's
sword, with his small cuisse and belt, which are today on show, are also adorned
with concentric circles in silver thread and the usual motto: " only God is the conqueror ". The handles of shields and other military and domestic objects were
also embroidered in coloured silks. The embroidery known as *cadeneta* or chain-
stitch, usually on linen, was a common domestic art among the women of Granada, as was the making of bone-lace.

Carpets played an important part in the decoration and furnishing of the Moslem
household in Granada. They were used, not only for covering the flooring of
baked mud slabs, which were sometimes glazed, but also the walls, giving even
the poorest room an opulent and comfortable appearance. Indeed, the plaster-
work on the walls of the Alhambra is only a permanent tapestry. The floors of
the mosques were usually covered with esparto mats, the luxurious carpets being
reserved for the private oratories of kings and noblemen. But there were also
small prayer-mats, so that the ordinary Moslems could be sure of the purity of
the spot in which they said their daily prayers. In the Archaeological Museum

53. Detail of a Moorish amphora, Toledo.

145

of Granada there is an example of the carpet-making of the Nasrid period. Although it has deteriorated somewhat, the characteristics of its manufacture are easily distinguished. It is made of wool and is decorated with knots, medallions, stars etc., coloured in white, two shades of blue, green and yellow on a red background. It was made by the so-called Persian method, which involved knotting the woof thread around one warp thread and passing it behind the next.

The Andalusian craft next in importance after weaving, was leather-work. Among the best known types of leather were the cordwains or cordovans, so called because they came from Cordoba; these were made from tanned goat-skins; the embossed leathers were made from tanned sheepskin which was then coloured and gilded. These leathers were used in Málaga and Granada for the manufacture of all kinds of objects: caparisons for horses, sword-belts and other appendages of apparel, weapon-pads and scabbards. Very few of these products have survived, despite the fact that they were exported in large quantities to Christian Spain.

The Nasrid ceramic industry can be divided into two main groups: one produced domestic pottery and the other opulent, gilded porcelain. Characteristic of this craft were the disproportionately wide necks of the vessels produced. In the vicinity of the Alhambra there was apparently a deep-red mineral clay, used for making thin pots that were especially good for keeping water cool. The Nasrid potters continued making the vessels, decorated in relief, both glazed and unglazed, that had originated in the Almohad period. They were usually large vases with wing-shaped handles. These were made from a reddish clay and decorated with geometric designs and Kufic inscriptions, as well as animal figures such as dogs, giraffes, monkeys and peacocks. Another common type of pottery was dark green and decorated with a manganese glaze on the inside. It usually takes the form of a pan or deep plate, almost always unglazed on the outside. Málaga, too, had a thriving pottery industry, the products of which bear the name *Malika*, written in Arabic. According to one theory, this inscription gave rise to the term " majolica " used by the Italians for glazed and decorated pottery. Blue and gilt vases were numerous, but the fragments that have survived are blue only, having lost their original gilt. It may have been these fragments that inspired the present-day potters of Granada to use blue shades, the craft being known as " blue pottery ". The Alhambra Museum possesses a large vase of red clay, hand-moulded except for the neck, and decorated in blue and gold.

Scarcely any examples of glass-making of the Nasrid epoch have survived, undoubtedly because of the fragility of the material. A few pieces of moulded and enamelled glass have been discovered in the Alhambra, with cursive lettering in white enamel standing out against a blue or wine-coloured background.

Ivory was in great demand in Granada for the manufacture of various types of objects and for the decoration of the handles of swords, daggers, rapiers and crossbows. Among the few articles of luxury to be found even in wealthy households, were a large number of chests (*ills.* 24, 25 and 26, and *pp.* 46 and 47). These were usually rectangular, with pyramidal lids. Their decoration consisted of punched open-work in black and gold, together with motifs such as the usual cursive inscriptions praising the owners of the chests; human figures either playing musical instruments, or drinking or sitting; animals; circles; knots; *attawriq* foliage and rosettes. The locks and fittings were usually of latten or gilded copper.

Two magnificent examples of the work of the ebony craftsmen survive: the leaves of the closet door (now in the Alhambra Museum) and the sceptre of the Nasrid

Sultans, which was later used as a staff by Cardinal Cisneros. The leaves of the door are covered in a meticulous and fine interlaced marquetry, which is made of tiny pieces of wood, silver and bone. In some places in the design, these pieces are glued on, instead of being inlaid. The staff or sceptre must have been made in the mid-fourteenth century. It is almost sixty inches long, with a core of iron wrapped in hemp fibres which are encircled by cylinders of ebony and rings of brass.

Typical Moorish tile mosaic and stucco wall decoration.

There was also in Granada a thriving metal industry, in brass, copper, iron etc. Of the examples that survive, the most important is the handsome lamp that once belonged to the Royal Mosque in the Alhambra, now preserved in the National Archaelogical Museum in Madrid. It is cast in bronze and adorned with chiselled open-work. It is suspended from a rod decorated with open-work pommels, which diminish in size as they descend. Its shade is shaped like the base of a cone, and bears several cursive inscriptions of the Nasrid motto " only God is the conqueror ", which is repeated on the pommels.

Jewellery and goldsmiths' work were extremely popular in the Granada Court. Al-Khatib tells us that women at that time were rather fat and short, and went about weighed down by trinkets. Ladies of nobility or importance adorned themselves with rich necklaces, bracelets, ear-rings, beads, anklets of pure gold and silver, and other precious ornaments for the feet. The Moors of Granada showed great skill in making such jewellery as well as in cutting and polishing precious stones, especially rubies and emeralds. It is regrettable that we scarcely have any examples of their work, which, because of the value of the materials, was broken up or melted down. Furthermore, since Moslems are buried stripped of their jewellery, the tombs have not provided examples of this art. Neither is it likely that the treasures that generations of Andalusians have supposed hidden in the walls or floors of the palaces would not have come to light by now. All we possess are some examples of wrought gold on the hilts of weapons and filigreed and enamelled silver on the chapes and handles of scabbards. In the Museum of Granada there are some bangles of engraved and hammered gold plate. These were worn by the women of Granada on their wrists and on their ankles.

It goes almost without saying that weapons were the commonest product of the Granada workshops. There are many examples of swords, daggers, poniards etc., some intended for warfare and therefore decorated simply, others with extremely rich ornamentation for Court festivals and processions. The Archaeological Museum of Granada possesses a crossbow with a stock, which has bronze inlay work with *attawriq* designs of inset ivory. This is what is known as *ataijía* or damaskeen work. For the decoration of other weapons, many kinds of material were used: ivory, gold, silver, horn, iron etc.; as well as different techniques: damaskeening proper (gold thread inlaid on iron), niello work (inlay of silver sulphide), fired gilding, enamel, filigree work, repoussé etc.

From all this detail of the minor decorative arts of the Nasrid people, there emerges a general artistic tendency that the inhabitants of Granada still possess: a meticulousness, a delicacy, a preoccupation with minutiae. It may be that these small objects reveal more of their character and taste than the great monuments which they have left us.

The Albaicín Quarter

This mass of delicately wrought *objets d'art* took shape in the hill suburbs, whose inhabitants depended almost entirely on the requirements of the Nasrid Court for their livelihood. These suburbs are as congested and jumbled as an antheap, and their streets are lined with stalls where the craftsmen work under the eyes of the purchaser or the passer-by. The German traveller Hieronymus Münzer visited Granada when the Albaicín was still inhabited by the Moslems who opted to carry on their business there after the city had capitulated to the Christians. Münzer says that the houses were minute—minuteness being always a characteristic of Granada—and so huddled together that the gables of the houses touched across the narrow streets. The houses had wooden front doors, covered with wooden studs, in African style. A later writer, Luis del Mármol y Carvajal, author of the *History of the Morisco Rebellion*, written at the end of the

54. Niche in carved marble forming part of the entrance of the Sala de la Barca in the Alhambra.

55. Stone lions at the pool of the Partal, in front of the Torre de las Damas in the Alhambra.

56. Fountain in the gardens of the Generalife.

55

56

sixteenth century, very close to the events it describes, asserts that many streets were too narrow for horses.

Many of the Moors and Moriscos who lived on the hills surrounding the Alhambra later began to disperse. Some of the streets were widened a little to allow the Christian families to build their *cármenes* which sometimes covered an area four or five times that covered by a Moorish house. But the general appearance and the daily life of the area retained much of their Moorish character. The persistence of Moslem features is perhaps most noticeable in the complex maze of lanes and tiny squares that forms the Albaicín quarter. The well-informed French traveller and author, Jean Sermet, gives us this account of it:

" As soon as we enter it, we seem to have left Europe behind us. Its surrounding walls are still almost intact, and we find our way in through the Puerta de Elvira with its low arch. Inside, we are plunged into a labyrinth of steep lanes and flights of steps. We must take care not to slip on the cobblestones. Ill-shapen squares and narrow lanes, which have scarcely changed in appearance since the day they were visited by Münzer, lead off a sloping and tortuous main street. Here and there, we catch a glimpse of a Morisco or Mudejar house, a half-hidden *patio*, a water-cistern, even an ancient minaret. As we climb upwards, human noises seem to subside. We come across a tiny silent square which is surrounded by jasmine-topped walls, uneven in height and giving access to four different streets. All is silence and the air is filled with the penetrating fragrance of flowers. A beggar passes slowly by. Whose pity can he hope to rouse in this seemingly blind and closed world? Let us climb further. Now in the sunshine, let us pause in an open space; at the far end, near the wall, stands the Upper Chapel of San Miguel. There, about a dozen Andalusians lie in a row in anonymous sleep. Why should they gaze over the Vega, as we do? They know it too well and see it every day; moreover, the sun hurts the eyes; it is wiser to sleep. What of their daily needs? The Lord will provide. These lads probably do not belong to the Albaicín; the suburb has kept its character of a busy, noisy hive, where serious tasks are carried out by respectable craftsmen, just as in the time of the Moors: a small and compact village that gains its livelihood from work in bronze, esparto, wrought iron, marquetry and Alpujarra fabrics; and in the gardens and *patios* hard-working girls do magnificent embroidery on pieces of linen for a few farthings. Clearly this is the Moorish quarter still! "

Jean Sermet has completely grasped the Morisco atmosphere amid this setting of gardens and *cármenes*, over which rise the minarets of the mosques that are now converted into churches. One makes one's way through the narrow streets, stumbling along the rough slopes between the whitewashed walls. They resemble country lanes and their narrowness adds to their character. The quarter contains many Morisco houses, and even some noble palaces of the Nasrid period are in a reasonable state of repair. The whole of the Albaicín seems designed for the close enjoyment of nature; its many gardens, situated on the side of the hill, provide excellent views. The houses are generally of a modest kind, though many of the *cármenes* have a rather lordly aspect. The general plainness of the exteriors clearly derives from Arabic customs and preferences—they always showed more interest in the natural setting than in architectural extravagance. Since they have many customs and tastes in common with one another, the inhabitants of the Albaicín live together in close intimacy, this being partly forced upon them

57. Detail of the fountain in the Patio de los Leones.

58. Coupled-arched window set under the overhanging gable of the Patio de los Arrayanes; it is surrounded by an inscription of lines by Ibn Zamrak in praise of Mohammed V.

by the crampedness of their quarter; one cannot discern great social or economic distinctions among them.

To sum up, the Albaicín has a functional harmony that is perfect from the urban point of view. Its streets have the same objective as its gardens, and the tiny arbours provide pleasant spots, for rest and conversation, amid an ever-present aroma of flowers and trees, rising from the whitewalled gardens. Here, archaeology is not a dry study of the cold ruins of past civilizations, but rather forms part of an extremely lively way of life. This is the continuity we have mentioned. Although the houses and streets have undergone changes, they still possess their essential Morisco spirit.

On top of the Albaicín slope stands the old Alcazaba, probably built on the site of the Roman city of Illiberis. In Moorish times there must still have existed a number of Roman and Visigothic fortifications. But the Arabs undoubtedly destroyed most of these constructions, of which no trace now remains except in the entrance to the quarter. The area was later re-walled, with the Alcazaba in the centre of the enclosure. It is this fort that al-Khatib calls the Alcazaba Cadima or old fort, to distinguish it from the new fort built in the Alhambra enclosure. The old fort was constructed in 765 A.D. by the *wali* or governor of Elvira (Granada's neighbouring town), Hasan ben Abd al-Rahman al-Djeibaini, who apparently did not complete the work on it. Later, some additions were made: the first by King Habbus ben Ziri (reigned 1020-1037), and the second by his son and successor Badis (reigned 1037-1073). The latter also built a palace bearing his name in the Alhambra. Now only parts of the towers and walls of the old Alcazaba survive, apart from some old foundations that have since had houses built over them.

The Albaicín spread itself from the old Alcazaba towards the hill of San Miguel on one side, and between the Gate of Guadix and the Gate of the Alcazaba on the other. Although the name Albaicín seems to come from the refugees from Baeza who settled there, as we have pointed out, other investigators, beginning with al-Khatib himself, have said that it means " hilly quarter " or " quarter of the falconers ". In earlier times the name was reserved for only part of the suburb that now bears it; but slowly the name began to be used for the group of suburbs that stretches to the lower part of the city.

At one time the Albaicín was almost a separate city, and one of the most important centres of Granada life. Its importance is shown by the fact that it possessed thirty mosques, each with its public water-cisterns and fountains, many of which still survive. Seven years after the quarter was founded, its population swelled to almost thirty thousand, because of the arrival of the Moors who fled from Úbeda. Its inhabitants lived in small, ugly houses, which were clean inside, however, each having piped connections to the main supply of drinking water and to the main sewers. The historian Bermúdez de Pedraza asserts that the quarter had as much importance as the whole of the rest of the city, and its inhabitants were so warlike and unruly that they would scour the surrounding countryside in search of booty, in razzias or *algaras* (raids). The extent of the Albaicín's influence in the affairs of the Kingdom of Granada can be seen from the way its inhabitants took part in the revolts that marked the last years of the Sultanate; at times the suburb was the stronghold of rivals to the throne, as Boabdil found.

The population of the Albaicín further increased after the Christian Conquest, because the Moriscos, or baptized Moors, were sent there willy-nilly, and it

Stucco wall decoration with Arabic inscription.

became the Moorish quarter, segregated from the rest of the city. Later, the quarter often resisted the impositions of later Christian monarchs and its streets were frequently the scene of uprisings. It was there that the Morisco Rebellions, which led to the final expulsion from Spain of the majority of Moriscos, broke out in 1499 and 1568. It was then that the quarter went into decline, its leading citizens having been deported to Africa. The famous arts and crafts of the suburb also declined. It is true that the Christians carried on the traditional crafts, but they never reached the peak of achievement of the earlier period. The Albaicín's population continued to diminish and many of the houses became derelict. The result was that at the beginning of the seventeenth century there were only a few thousand poverty-stricken inhabitants. The situation was so bad that in 1620 there was a royal decree for the repopulation of the suburb. This was ineffective, however, and at the beginning of the eighteenth century there was a population of only thirteen hundred. As the modern city rapidly grew, the Albaicín suffered a further decline; its crafts very nearly disappeared and many of its ancient buildings fell into ruin. Despite everything, the quarter preserves some of its original character, as we have indicated.

The present population of the Albaicín is not entirely proletarian: at the gloomy cross-roads rise the walls of the *cármenes* or lordly villas, set between the tiny houses of the populace. The gardens of these villas are concealed by high whitewashed walls, over which peep the tops of dark cypresses and the hanging fronds of trailing plants. The houses of this quarter have an air of minute and complete intimacy, as has everything in Granada. The small squares, the mysterious corners, the smell of concentrated humanity and full-blown jasmine grip one's heart with emotion and joy. From the narrow streets and secret gardens of the Albaicín one can glimpse the red walls of the Alhambra; and the palace quietly dreaming of its glorious past, gazes down on the mesh of innumerable lanes that form the Albaicín.

The lay-out of its streets and squares must be almost exactly the same as in the Morisco period, and the artistic achievements of that epoch are clearly visible in many of the houses and *cármenes* of the suburb. The austere and humble appearance of these houses bears witness to the character of the conquered Moslems, who carried on their traditional crafts in the shadow of the Alhambra, symbol of their lost power. Today in the narrow streets and sad *patios* there is an air of exile, which has been unconsciously inherited from the past. Gallego Burín says of the inhabitants, " their intense glances and the timbre of their voices contain evocations of the past, like those hidden in the depths of the water-cisterns, which are sunlit and picturesque on the surface." There are many traces of the Moors also in the complex maze of streets in the Albaicín. But it is difficult to discover them in a methodical way. It is almost preferable to wander aimlessly, in the hope of chancing upon the points of interest one is sure to find at every turning. In addition to the various churches, each of which has its own history and artistic treasures, there are innumerable houses of definite Morisco origin, with nearby cisterns and remains of ancient fortifications and mosques: among these houses are no. 2, Calle de Yanguas, no. 14, Calle de San Martín, no. 27, Calle de San Luis, nos. 1, 19, 28 and 37, Calle del Agua, no. 19, Calle de la Mina, no. 22, Calle de Fátima, no. 28, Calle de la Verónica and no. 32, Calle de Pardo. In a secluded corner stands the Ermita de San Miguel—St Michael is the patron saint of the gipsies of the Sacromonte. This hermitage was originally called the Aceituno (" olive-tree "), and consisted of a tower built on the site of an early Christian church, where an olive-tree once grew. According to legend, this olive-tree was very famous among the Arabs for its capacity of bearing flowers and ripened fruit every twenty-four hours.

In another corner of the Albaicín there still stands a Moslem palace called the Daralhorra or House of the Queen, which belonged to the Nasrid royal family. This palace later formed part of the group of buildings which the Catholic Kings gave to the nearby Monastery of Santa Isabel la Real. Not long ago the monastery sold it to the Spanish Government, who have carried out restorations and saved it from ruin. The palace dates from about the middle of the fifteenth century and consists of a courtyard with porticos and arcades, a hall decorated with arches, painted ceilings and a pleasant balcony. Not far from this palace stood the *al-kasr* of the first dynasty of Granada, that of the Zirids, which was called the Alcázar of Badis or the Casa del Gallo (House of the Cockerel). It has disappeared without trace, but seems to have extended as far as the present-day Plaza de San Miguel el Bajo and the tenement known as the Casa de la Lona (House of the Canvas).

The Albaicín quarter has another attraction: in the sunny and peaceful square in front of the new Church of St Nicholas, there is a magnificent vantage-point; indeed, it is the best in Granada, because it offers the fullest view of the Alhambra. From there we can see the proud crimson towers rising in harmonious contrast with the dark green of the wooded slopes of Sabika, against the unique background of the snowy peaks of the Sierra Nevada.

59. The Puerta de la Justicia, the main entrance to the Alhambra enclosure. The open hand on the keystone of the arch probably symbolizes the five precepts of the Koran: fasting, alms-giving, prayer, pilgrimage to Mecca and belief in the oneness of God.

The Lower City and the Sacromonte

After the Christian occupation, Granada lost nothing of its splendour. The fusion of Christian and Moslem elements was firmly established, although it later weakened considerably. Certainly, there was a peaceful co-existence of the two peoples for a long period. The result of this was that in the lower part of the city, beneath the walls of the Alhambra, the monuments exhibit a harmonious intermingling of both styles. Even in the suburbs where Moslem influence was least felt, the Christian monuments often possess a Moslem feature where it is least expected.

The lower part of the city is modern and Christian; the upper part is ancient and Moorish. They constitute the Granada of Islam and the Granada of the Reconquest, separated as much in space as in time. Of course, these are vague generalizations: in many places the two civilizations have inter-penetrated and even fused. Within the very enclosure of the Alhambra, beside the Arabic palaces, the Holy Roman Emperor Charles V had his palace built, as well as a fountain in pure renaissance style just below the Puerta de la Justicia of the Sultan Yusuf. In the lower city, along the street of the Catholic Kings, the city's main artery, are the ancient Moorish hostelry now called the Casa del Carbón, with its horse-shoe arch, and the narrow lanes called the Zacatín and the Alcaicería, where once the bazaars of Moslem Granada were concentrated.

The Cathedral stands approximately on the spot where the Great Mosque was situated. The busy square called the Bibarrambla still has the same name and character that it had during the last years of the Sultanate, and its entrance near the Cathedral and the Zacatín has not changed. This vast square was once the scene of tourneys, joustings and all sorts of contests, and, as its Arabic name indicates (Gate of the Sand), was then on the banks of the Darro at the point where it left the city to join the Genil on the Vega. Since then the Darro has been diverted and channelled along the street called the Carrera del Darro; the river then passes underground below the street of the Catholic Kings and the street of the Puerta Real. This latter street was nearly destroyed in 1951 when the river was in spate and broke through its arched cover. Once, the river traversed the city and was crossed by picturesque bridges; the city's hygiene, however, has greatly benefited from the underground channelling. Apart from this major change and a few others of a minor nature, the city can be recognized perfectly well in a Huefnagel engraving of 1503, which is kept in the Emperor's Rooms in the Alhambra (the same rooms were occupied centuries later by the American writer Washington Irving, who was enraptured by the city of the sultans).

The lower city is full of artistic, or rather, historic, treasures. The enormous Cathedral is impressive more for its size than its architecture. It is one of three famous renaissance churches built in the first quarter of the sixteenth century, the others being in Jaén and Málaga. Not one of the three was finally completed until the seventeenth and eighteenth centuries. The religious heart of Granada is not to be found in the vast Cathedral but in the Royal Chapel which is annexed to it. It is not the baroque exterior of this chapel (which is in Spanish *plateresco* style, with overtones of the even more elaborate Portuguese *manuelino* decoration) that moves the people of Granada to Christian fervour, but rather the relics that lie within. Beyond an opulently wrought screen stand the tombs of the Catholic Kings, who with their capture of Granada brought the whole Peninsula under their sway. Nearby are the tombs of their daughter Joan the Mad and her

60. The ceiling in *mocárabe* stucco-work in the Sala de los Abencerrajes in the Alhambra. On the walls, *attawriq* designs and religious inscriptions.

husband Philip the Fair. Beneath the handsome sepulchres, the lead coffins are closely guarded and can be seen from a staircase. The sovereigns' wooden statues, which are not very flattering, flank the reredos that depicts with great realism scenes from the Christian Reconquest. The Reliquary contains some particularly emotive mementoes: the banner of the Catholic Kings, Ferdinand's crown and sceptre, and Isabella's prayer-book and her looking-glass, now made into a paten. As far as pure art is concerned, the chapel contains a magnificent surprise: a fine collection of Flemish primitive paintings, donated by Charles V in memory of his grandparents. All these relics bear witness to the beginnings of modern Granada.

The sixteenth century saw a new splendour in Granada as in the whole of Andalusia, by then enriched by the discovery of America. There are many, but little-known, relics of the Renaissance and early Golden Age in the city. The grandeur of this period is not reflected so much in the Cathedral or the Palace of Charles V as in the Church of St Hieronymus, which dates from 1547. It is a national monument but has an empty and forlorn air; even so, it possesses an incomparable reredos. Another building well worth visiting is the Audiencia, or law court, in the Plaza Nueva. In addition to these, many façades and colonnades, glimpsed suddenly from a busy street, will reveal the artistic tendency peculiar to sixteenth-century Granada, where Christians and Moors intermingled, forming a rich Mudejar community. According to Mármol the historian, Morisco dances accompanied the Corpus Christi processions at that time. Could Granada have brought about a complete symbiosis of East and West, by which Spain might have experienced the most curious twist in its history? This is a question that will never be answered, because this brilliant experiment was scarcely begun. The insurrection of the Moriscos in 1568 and the expulsion that followed, forthwith erased all the best Islamic elements.

From that moment, Granada dedicated itself to Christianity with great fervour. A cross stands below the old Plaza de Toros on the spot where the Duke of Gandía was converted. San Juan de Dios preached sermons and founded a hospital; he was canonized in 1630 and a basilica, in classical style, erected in his honour, later received the Lateran privileges. There was also much devotion to Our Patron Lady of the Sorrows. The Jesuits contributed austerely grandiose buildings to the University, which was founded in 1526. It is the Jesuits who now operate the climatological and seismographical observatory at the Cartuja. In later times the religious fervour lost its impetus. Granada, having become a city of wealth, became a city of Baroque. The seventeenth century witnessed a large number of opulent extravagances: the hall of San Juan de Dios glitters with stained glass and silver; the Cartuja dazzles with marble, gold and sculptures. These centuries, however, are the great monumental period of Christian Granada.

The nineteenth century enjoyed destruction: in 1884, Gómez Moreno wrote a *Brief account of the monuments and works of art lost to Granada in this century*. With a *nouveau-riche* mentality and an eagerness to create great modern things, the people of Granada tore down the Mosque quarter in order to lay out a network of streets all at right angles to one another. Certainly, the aim was to improve these streets: in one of them can be seen the house where Théophile Gautier stayed in 1843, and the house where *The Present Empress of France* was written (it bears a commemorative tablet dated 1867). Granada and Grenoble were the first two European cities to install electric lighting—a sign of wealth and progress. It is clear

Stucco wall decoration.

however that these changes caused Granada to lose some of its original character.

Outside the Cathedral there is a maze of narrow streets, full of small souvenir shops. This is the Alcaicería, once the Moorish silk market, which has remained unchanged, apart from the removal of the large doors that formerly enclosed it. There are now over two hundred shops, filled with all the products of the present-day crafts of Granada. In the Plaza del Cabildo in this suburb, there stands the Madraza, the ancient Arabic university built by Yusuf I in the fourteenth century. This building now possesses few Moorish features, though at one time it had a fine portal adorned with *attawriq* designs on marble. Soon after the Reconquest, the structure became the first Christian town hall. It later underwent all kinds of alterations, most of which naturally followed the baroque traditions so typical of Granada.

The Moslem building in the lower city that has retained most of its original character is the Casa del Carbón. Under Moorish rule, it was the *alhóndiga*, or public granary. Its main entrance has a horse-shoe arch, built entirely of brick and partly decorated with *attawriq* patterns. The entrance-hall has *mocárabe* vaulting and leads to a square *patio* with a central fountain and surrounding galleries. At the back of the galleries there are several small rooms that once housed the merchants and traders who had travelled from distant lands to conduct business in the city. This inn has the same lay-out as the African *fondaks,* the Byzantine caravanserais and the Asiatic *hans.* It dates from the first half of the fourteenth century and is the best example of its kind in Spain, despite the alterations it underwent, especially in the sixteenth century, when it was used for several years as a yard for the performance of plays; it was there that the works of Lope de Rueda and many other playwrights were staged.

Another interesting building in the lower part of the city is the Casa de los Tiros (House of the Cannons). It is a typical Christian residence of Granada and is preserved intact. Between the turrets that surmount the structure loom the muzzles of the culverins after which the building is named. It dates from the sixteenth century and formerly belonged to the Granada Venagas family, which was supposed to have descended from the kings of Granada. The façade bears a coat of arms consisting of a sword and a heart, with the motto " He commandeth me ". Inside, there is a fine entrance-hall with a ceiling of Gothic beams, on which the original painted decoration still survives. There is a *patio* typical of Granada and a gilded room lined with paintings. Like most of the noble houses of the city, the building is a virtual museum of the crafts of the district.

This part of Granada is full of baroque extravagance: it is to be found in most of the churches, in the new University and in many other buildings. The Carrera del Darro leads to the most evocative parts of Granada. In the Plaza Nueva stands the Real Cancillería (Royal Chancery), the design of which exhibits a clear Italian influence. It possesses considerable grandeur, despite its austere decoration which is most surprising in a city where hardly a space is left unadorned. On the Carrera del Darro itself, are the Bañuelos or Moorish baths, which have recently been restored. There is also the Casa del Castril, where the Archaeological Museum finds rather inadequate accommodation for its many prehistoric, Iberian, Roman, Visigothic and Arabic exhibits. The Carrera del Darro finally joins the picturesque Paseo de los Tristes; nearby is the Casa del Chapiz, a Morisco building that manifests a fusion of Arabic and Christian influences in a manner characteristic of the city.

At the outskirts of the city stands the Monasterio de la Cartuja. This structure is surrounded by high walls and its portal is in *plateresco* style, which was inspired by the Renaissance and preceded the baroque extravagance of the *churrigueresco* style. The great staircase of this portal leads to a sort of vestibule, where there are two small altars and two canvases by Friar Juan Sánchez Cotán, who was a monk of this monastery. One of the paintings portrays the Flight into Egypt and the other the Baptism of Christ. Another monk, Friar José Vázquez, carried out the inlay-work in shell, ivory and fine wood of the door that stands between the two altars; this laborious task must have taxed his monastic patience to the utmost. The choir of this monastery has an over-elaborate ornamentation, much of which is not in the best taste. Behind the altar and presbytery is the sanctum sanctorum, where one aisle is lined with paintings, including a Madonna once attributed to Cano, but now known to be the work of Bocanegra. There are also four more paintings by the mystic Friar Juan Sánchez Cotán.

The sanctum, now used as the sacrarium of the church, is a richly decorated room in baroque style and is the work of Francisco Hurtado Izquierdo, who executed it in the first decades of the eighteenth century. The tabernacle is made of inlaid stone, with Solomonic columns and pilasters and a domed canopy, and is faced with the seven Carthusian stars in wrought bronze and wood. It contains some statues of angels sculpted by José Risueño. On the right is a door leading to the sacristy. There is one room in the sacristy where everything, from the columns to the cornices, not to mention the capitals and the vaulting, is a dazzling interplay of colours, arabesques and minutiae. This is the style known as *churrigueresco*, which was the apotheosis of Spanish Baroque. The whole of the eighteenth century is crammed into this room: Lanjarón marbles, fervently sculpted stone, tiny looking-glasses, plaster-work like peaked cream, inlay-work of silver, ivory, shell, lignum vitae and ebony. José María Pemán has said of this decorative chaos, " It is like a motionless architectural earthquake ".

This tendency for ornamental extravagance became so common in Granada that baroque and *churrigueresco* were frequently described as " the Granada style ". Once more we can see the Nasrid tradition in operation. The artists of Granada lacked a Medieval Christian background; thus, when they reacted against neo-Classicism, they turned to baroque and to the *attawriq* designs of the earlier Moslem plaster-workers. As we have already pointed out, the city's main artistic trend continued to be a love of minute elaboration. Granada is filled with tiny looking-glasses, minute, doll-like statuettes of saints and plaster lozenges. Even in popular speech, nearly every word bears the diminutive suffix *-ico*.

* * *

The most picturesque part of Granada today is the strange Sacromonte quarter, where the gipsies live in their sumptuous caves. Little now remains of the gipsy life of the Romantic prints, sketched by Gustave Doré and admired by Gautier. Nevertheless, in this suburb of hills and caves, one can still admire proud representatives of the race whose mysterious origin has yet to be fully explored. There are still many haughty women in gay and colourful finery.

The road to Sacromonte climbs a steep mountain slope and is edged with cactuses, agaves, prickly pears and other desert plants. The caves are near the road and are brilliant with whitewash, giving an air of gaiety to the wild scenery. At first sight one might think that these people were forced to live in caves because of poverty. That was not the case. One needs only to enter one of these picturesque dwellings to see their comfort and luxury. The walls are decorated with shining copper utensils, pottery, prints and coloured glass. Guitars and castanets provide an almost continuous musical background. The suburb will be better understood if it is visited in daylight, although as far as entertainment is concerned it is at its best at night, with its famous *zambras*. In these festivals, amid the tumultuous cries of the onlookers, the noise of the music, the frantic

FROM THE ALBAICÍN
TO THE SACROMONTE
clicking of fingers and the almost pathetic contortions of the dancers bring to mind (if the *zambra* is authentic) the ritual nature of this choreographic form. The despairing rhythms are undulating at times and broken at others. The whole spirit of a nomadic race, probably of Egyptian or Hindu origin (both have been suggested), manifests itself in these dances: the gipsy tango, the wedding *cachucha*, the bolero, the fandango etc., punctuated by the dry hand claps and the quaking, broken voices of the *cantaores*. This primitive music, which has a pathetic background similar to that of the traditional jazz of America, has provided the inspiration and the aesthetic model for many Spanish composers, such as Falla.

THE RED PALACE
OF THE NASRID SULTANS

In the whole of Spain there is probably no hill or mountain so steeped in history as the Sabika or Assabika, which rises over the shady ravine of the Darro and the dazzling spread of the Vega. Here ancient Illiberis may have stood; here the Roman legions of the Empire fortified their *castrum*; here traces were left by the Goths, the early Moslem invaders, the Berber tribes elated with fanaticism and greed, and the Christian Reconquerors. Zawi, the first Zirid king, and Mohammed Banu 'l-Ahmar, the founder of the Nasrid Dynasty, in their turn gazed in astonishment at the red walls and wooded slopes, and on the summit they constructed the halls and residences that were to serve as a magnificent home for their descendants and successors: the new Alcazaba, the Alhambra, the Generalife... Enchanted by this tranquil and ecstatic height, Ibn Zamrak, one of the greatest poets of Islamic Spain, composed these spacious lines:

" From Sabika's esplanade extend your gaze: the city is a lady betrothed to the hill.

Look at the streams attending the groves, like hosts pouring liquor for their guests.

Sabika is the crown on Granada's brow, and the stars of heaven yearn to be its jewels;

And the Alhambra, may God protect it, is the central ruby of its crown."

The pleasure-loving and convivial Moorish poets of al-Andalus, full of high-flown eulogies, never tired of addressing fervent hymns of praise to Sabika and its red palace. And indeed, in that high palace, enclosed by a wall almost a mile and a quarter long, in the midst of forests of slim columns, amid so much filigree work, by the quiet pools and in the fresh atmosphere of those halls that are like ethereal grottoes, there still seem to flit shades of heroic deeds, tragic events, mysterious decadent pleasures and steely clashes. Here, in this silent room, one can conjure up the veiled silhouette of an earthly houri; there, by the sun-reddened water of a stream, it is not difficult to sense the presence of an assassin lying in wait for a rival in love or politics. Noble and heroic deeds took place within these walls, as well as unbridled love affairs, feverish acts of revenge, uncontrollable feuds. This hill and its buildings have witnessed the pageant of many centuries and neither the subduing effect of time, nor the destructive anger of man in battle, nor even the long years of neglect that followed the glorious period of the Alhambra, have been able to rob these palaces, gardens and unique walls of their power of evocation—a power that survives because of the refined sensitivity of a decadent race and the exceptional natural scene in which that race found itself.

The right time to go up to the Alhambra is just after dawn or just before sunset. From the parapets or the windows of the towers one can see the city below, the detailed and complicated patchwork of houses, gardens, steep, narrow streets, secluded convents and tiny squares that look like the inner *patios* of houses. Like a fantastic animated map, the city and the plain are spread out before one's eyes in clear detail. And the sounds of the city are carried upwards faintly but clearly by the hollow gorge of the river below: the slow rhythmical motion of the carriages; the chatter of children; the twanging of a guitar or a piano; and above all the others, the hum of the Albaicín and the Sacromonte. From this confusion of elemental and distilled sounds, there suddenly emerges a perfectly distinguishable human voice. As José María Pemán has observed, it is " the voice of a housewife asking another on the next balcony for the loan of a mop or a bucket "; the voice ascends clear and clipped, but there is not the remotest chance of seeing its owner in some hidden corner far below.

Towering on Sabika, " Granada's crown ", the Alhambra and the Generalife are masterpieces virtually without imperfection, though built to human dimensions. The materials that went into these buildings are unbelievably insubstantial: simple plaster, bare wood, bricks and water, a great deal of water. It seemed impossible that these slight structures could survive, but they have lasted until our day. The builders had no wish for their constructions to endure forever. Yet they still stand, fresh and fragrant, although frequently repaired and restored.

The *alarifes* or architects who laid out these buildings and gardens had the ability to extract from common and inexpensive materials the maximum of comfort and beauty. The plasterwork is decorated in many colours and there is no doubt that the stucco-moulders who shaped it were endowed with an excessive sense of fantasy. Everything is fragile, improvised and minutely elaborated. The gardens and *patios* are generally planned on a small scale. Only the Patio de la Alberca and the Patio de los Arrayanes are at all large. The Patio de los Leones seems to have been intended as a place of recreation for a small family group. The pillars are extremely fine and slender. A supernatural air permeates this miraculous relic, which still stands unscathed, while many other equally old and more solid buildings have crumbled into dust.

History

The history of this hill, Sabika, and the network of buildings that are set on it, is long and complicated. A detailed account of it would fill many volumes, and the brief account that follows is a bare summary.

Because of the strategic position of this hill it can be supposed that, long before the Moslem invasion, there were already fortifications on it, which the Moors naturally rebuilt and enlarged, at the same time as they constructed the Alcazaba Cadima—now completely in ruins—on another hill on the opposite side of the river. It appears that they later added a bridge across the Darro to connect the two fortresses.

The shape of the walled enclosure is irregular; it is confined on the north by the valley of the Darro, on the south by Sabika and on the east by the slopes of Mount Rey Chico, all of which separate it from the Albaicín quarter, the

61. Fragment of an Arabic sundial. Height: 7⁷/₈".

62. Detail of the inscription on the marble tombstone of the founder of the Nasrid Dynasty. Height of tombstone 28¹/₈".

61

62

Monte Mauror on which the Torres Bermejas stand, and the Generalife on the slopes of Mount Sol, respectively. The name " Alhambra ", from the Arabic *kala hamra* (Red Castle), was clearly given to it because of the colour of the iron-bearing mud of which the bricks for its walls were made. But the historian al-Khatib attributes it to the fact that the original fort was rebuilt at night by the light of torches that threw a fantastic crimson glow over the scene. Any attempt to separate the military architecture of the towers and walls of this unique lay-out from the domestic architecture of the royal residence and the other minor buildings which it comprises, would disfigure a perfectly unified composition. The royal garden of the Generalife complements the Alhambra and the other buildings on the crimson hill of Sabika, the brow of which is surrounded by a strong turreted wall that closely follows its irregular contour. The main building axis of the Alhambra, which runs from south-east to north-west, measures nearly 810 yards in length and a little over 240 yards at its widest point, tapering sharply at either end. The new Alcazaba, a powerful fort with large towers, was built at the most north-westerly point of the hill, standing, as it were, on the prow of an enormous boat anchored between the sierra and the plain. In the central and lower section stands the royal palace, and distributed over the remainder of the enclosure are a large number of buildings of various kinds: the burial chapel of the monarchs, many houses, some of them palatial, where the court dignitaries lived; a royal mosque; the *Ceca* or Mint, the dwelling of servants and artisans who had workshops there for all the Court's material needs. Of the latter buildings, only part of the foundations and the general ground-plan remain.

From its earliest moment, the Alhambra was one of the centres of the civil strife that destroyed the Cordoban Caliphate. During those struggles, an Arab chieftain called Ibn Handum became obliged to take refuge in the fort that stood on the north side of the hill and he reconstructed it and improved its fortifications. This is the first firm fact known about the history of the place which until then seems to have been small and unimportant. This first enclosure, called Alcazaba or *alhisan*, was not enlarged and inhabited until some time afterwards, because the Zirid kings apparently established themselves on the opposite hill. But when these same kings built a new wall around the citadel in the eleventh century, the castle of the Alhambra became part of the original enclosure and was dominated by the Alcazaba. The hill was thus transformed into a fortress of great strategic value and, during the invasions of the Almoravids and the Almohads, it was once more the setting for bitter struggles on two outstanding occasions: the first was in 1144, when the chieftain Banu Hud was routed by the Almoravids; the second took place in 1161, when the army of the Almohad leader Abd al-Mumin destroyed the forces of the Almoravid leader Ibrahim ben Humushk.

Many years later, in 1238, the first Nasrid king Banu 'l-Ahmar decided to reside on the hill. It was he who started work on the Alcázar; in addition, he built new towers, re-fortified the walls, installed a good water-supply and provided food stores and military supply depôts. This work was continued by his son Mohammed II, and by his successor, Mohammed III, who built a bath and the great mosque. The kings who followed probably confined their activities to decorating what their predecessors had constructed, until Yusuf I and his son, Mohammed V, whose reigns stretched over the last three quarters of the fourteenth century, improved the earlier structures and added new buildings that include most of those now standing. These two kings, apart from strengthening the de-

63. The Alhambra Vase, the finest example of the " blue pottery " of Granada. Height 51½".

fences, enlarged and decorated the halls and towers, built new baths, added a ceremonial gateway to the Cuarto de Comares, restored the *décor* of the courtyard belonging to that hall and that of the courtyard of the Sala de la Barca, as well as building the Cuarto de los Leones. All that remains from the reigns that followed is the decoration of the Torre de las Infantas and possibly some part of the fortifications. As for the three towers called the Machuca, the Cautiva and the Candil, like the Puerta de la Justicia and the Oratorio del Partal, they were probably built in the reigns of Yusuf I and Mohammed V. The latter was also responsible for the completion of the Torre del Peinador, the Puerta del Vino and the remainder of the royal Alcázar. Finally, in the second half of the fifteenth century, some time before the Catholic Kings occupied Granada, a few more ramparts must have been added, but little else.

Once the Castilian monarchs had triumphed, they commanded that some work should be undertaken on the Alhambra in order to repair its walls and restore the *décor* of its rooms. They therefore appointed Don Íñigo López de Mendoza, Count of Tendilla, as governor of the citadel. From then onwards, the later counts of Tendilla held the same appointment. When Ferdinand and Isabella died, their daughter Joan I, to whom history has given the sad name of Joan the Mad, and their grandson the Holy Roman Emperor Charles V, continued to lavish every possible care on the ancient palace of Granada. Moreover, in 1526 the Emperor decided to reside in it for a time: he not only had renovated some of the rooms in the former Moorish Alcázar, but also ordered a renaissance palace to be built and enlarged the area now known as the Plaza de los Aljibes. When Philip II came to the throne, the maintenance of the Alhambra was not forgotten: money and workmen were sent to continue the work of restoration, which went on afterwards throughout the seventeenth century and was carried out with considerable deference to the style and spirit of the original.

The most difficult period in the Alhambra's history began in the eighteenth century during the War of the Spanish Succession, which involved the Hapsburgs and the Bourbons. The abandonment of the handsome citadel started when Philip V removed the Marquis of Mondéjar from the governorship of the palace, because he had favoured the Archduke of Austria in the conflict. The appointment was not filled and went into abeyance despite the protests of the people of Granada. The lamentable result of this apparent royal indifference or disdain was that the palace began to fall into decay. Only Charles III made any attempt to undertake the work of maintenance. This king, who was rightly called " the best mayor in Spain ", and who promoted so many public building projects throughout the kingdom, put the Alhambra in the care of the Judges of the Granada Chancery and in 1792 allotted them a small grant for that purpose.

The Alhambra's vicissitudes were not over, however. When Napoleon invaded the Peninsula at the beginning of the nineteenth century, the palace was converted into a military barrack and fort. Even so, it is said that the French generals, enthralled by their surroundings, carried out some maintenance and restoration. But this work was done in vain, because when the Napoleonic troops withdrew shortly afterwards, they blew up parts of the walls and towers. This destruction was made good by Ferdinand VII, who in 1830 assigned 50,000 *reales* for the purpose, and by the Queen Regent María Cristina. The historical importance of the Alhambra was recognized some years later, in 1870, when it was declared a national monument. Since then various funds have been allotted to it and it has been carefully preserved, first under the auspices of several State

64. Oil lamp in bronze.
Heigth 4¼"; length 9".

65. Delicate flask in glass, used
for perfumes or cosmetics.
Height 31½".

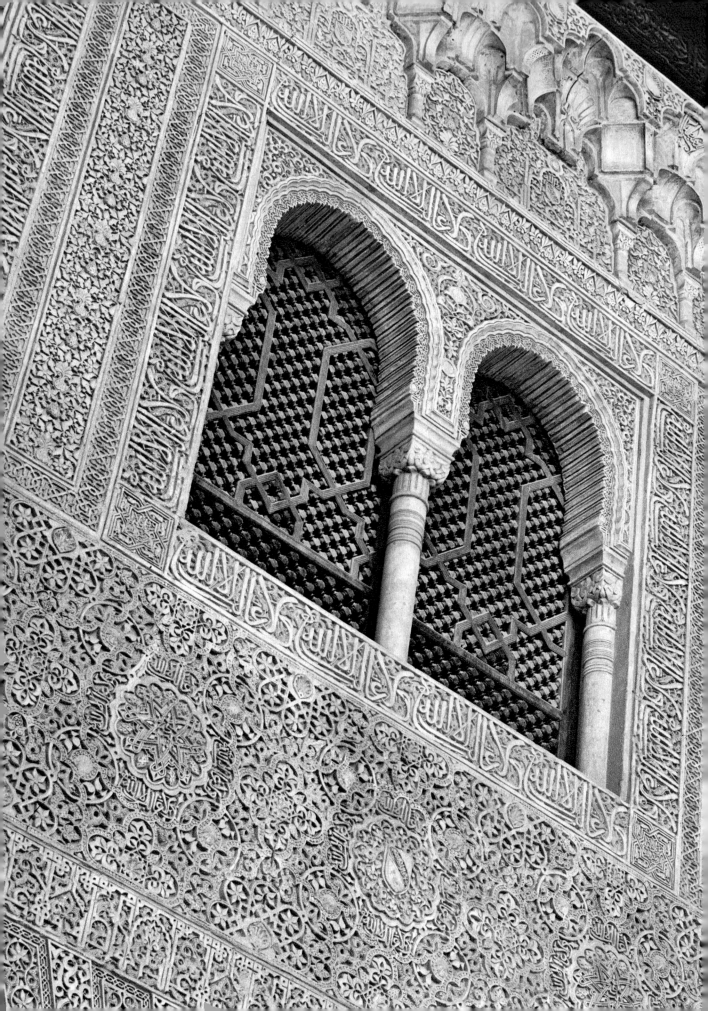

commissions and finally, from 1938 onwards, in the care of the Ministry of Education. Today the Alhambra, with all its artistic, sentimental and historical value, stands unscathed and its importance as a monument is recognized by those who are in charge of it.

The Palace

Although the name *Alhambra* is now applied to the whole group of buildings within the walled enclosure and sometimes to those outside as well, such as the Generalife, it should be observed that there are three sections which are distinct as much by their appearance and character as by their position on the hill. These three parts are: the new Alcazaba or military citadel, which rises on the highest point of Sabika; the Royal Palace, which is set in a hollow in the centre of the hill and which is separated from the Alcazaba by the Plaza de los Aljibes; and the upper Alhambra or village, which consisted of the dwellings, which have now mostly disappeared, of the courtiers and servants of the Nasrid Court. Of the three, the first section is the oldest, but the least known. The other two parts sprang up together in the shelter of the earlier defences, which must be studied in detail if the composition of the monument that was a fortress, palace and city at the same time—the best preserved monument of the Moslem domination of Spain and the outstanding representative of Arabic architecture in the Western world—is to be understood. It stands as the supreme expression of the Moorish art of Granada and comprises not only the achievements of an austere military architecture, but also civic buildings whose range includes all the components of a miniature civilization, for such was the Nasrid Court.

The best route from the city to the Alhambra and the other buildings on Sabika lies along the Cuesta de Gomeres, a slope apparently named after some Morisco family. This road starts in the Plaza Nueva in the centre of Granada and ultimately leads to the spot where once stood the Moorish *Bib Albushar* (Gate of Good News), also called *Bib Haudak* (Fosse Gate), which was set in one of the outer keeps of the city and constituted one of the main entrances to the Alhambra enclosure. Today on that same spot stands the Puerta de las Granadas, built in 1536 at the behest of the Emperor Charles V by the architect Pedro Machuca. The Tuscan columns of this gate support a semicircular arch, the triangular pediment of which is decorated with three symbolic open pomegranates, the heavy Imperial badge and some figures representing Peace and Plenty. It is odd that the main entrance to an enclosure crowded with Moslem relics and Oriental works of art should consist of a structure decorated in massive renaissance style. The tower, which is about thirty feet high and nine feet thick, is made of Escúzar stone and is bossed, in keeping with its rather crude design. Charles V's good intentions usually did not accord very well with artistic precision and harmony. His action in building this gateway to the Alhambra is similar to his well known and disastrous alteration of the Cordoban Mosque, which robbed it of its architectural purity and balance. His later public admission that these operations were a mistake was probably the result of a hint by someone more versed in the arts than he.

The Puerta de las Granadas is set in the wall that joins the Alcazaba to the Torres Bermejas, called "crimson" because of their colour, which stand on the western edge of Monte Mauror, site of the ancient ghetto, and which constituted the foremost line of defence of the enclosure. These towers are probably the oldest relics in the city and apparently date from the last years of the eighth

66. Part of the wall in the Patio del Mexuar in the Alhambra.

century and the first years of the ninth. The Torres Bermejas now consist of three towers and are reached by a gate added much later, in the sixteenth century, which has a horse-shoe arch. Until quite recently they belonged to the army and were used as a military prison. Emilio García Gómez said of them, " In Granada there is a secret palace; everyone talks of it but no one has seen it. It is called the Torres Bermejas."

The route continues upwards along a winding road flanked by dense woodlands. Through the dense foliage the tinkling of water is audible, but one scarcely can obtain a glimpse of it—the poet Manuel Machado called it " agua oculta que llora..." (" a secret, weeping water..."). The trees are mainly elms and black poplars. Branching water-channels cross the whole woodland and contribute to the delightful oasis effect, which is heightened by the contrast with the almost treeless streets and squares of the city below. This dense, murmuring wood covers a steep slope that descends to a neck between Sabika and Mauror. It is at its best in summer, because its trees are of the Nordic type, and in winter it is left bare by the falling leaves. But in summer its shade provides an incomparable coolness.

These enchanting woods which surround the Alhambra pose a curious problem: many historians have queried whether they were there when the palace was first inhabited. It does not seem likely, because the hill of Sabika was above all a strategic fort and the presence of trees would have been a hindrance, offering cover for ambushes at the foot of the walls. Furthermore, it would appear strange to deliberately surround a palace in which light and colour provide the main decorative effects, with that utterly Northern scenery, full of shadows, hidden gurgling streams and the melancholy song of nightingales. When Hieronymus Münzer visited Granada in 1494, two years after the Christian conquest of the city, he stated that at that time these slopes were occupied by a large Moslem cemetery. It should be remembered that the Moors always chose an area outside their walled enclosure and near the gates of the city for their burial grounds just as the Romans did before them. This fact appears to confirm Münzer's testimony, for which there was other contemporary support. Other historians tell us that, in the luxurious palace of the Nasrids, there were leafy bowers and vast gardens, but they always talk of them as being within the walls, never outside the palace proper. It has also been stated that we owe the present shady groves to General Wellington, who ordered, during his stay in Granada, that these groves should be planted or, at least, re-afforested.

Just outside the walls of the Alhambra is a large fountain built into the wall of an old square tower. Today it is known as the Pilar de Carlos V (The Basin of Charles V); earlier it was called the Pilar de las Cornetas (Basin of the Cornets). It is built of sandstone that has been delicately mellowed by the sun of several centuries. It was constructed some time between 1543 and 1545 by order of the Count of Tendilla to a design of Pedro Machuca, like the Puerta de las Granadas, and the design was carried out by the Italian Nicolao da Corte, in pure renaissance style with extremely rich ornamentation. Since it was dedicated to Charles V, the Imperial badge and arms were inscribed on the pediment; further down, three masks protrude from the stone, emitting water from their mouths. These three masks appear to symbolize the rivers of Granada, the Darro and Genil and the less well known Beiro.

The so-called Puerta de la Justicia is only a few yards from the Pilar de Carlos V. The modernist poet Salvador Rueda described this gate as " one of the most hand-

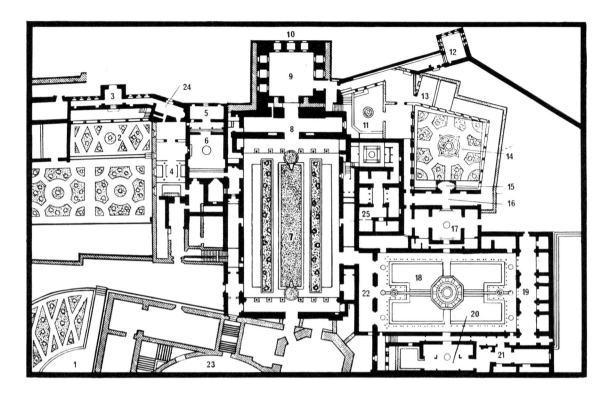

PLAN OF THE MOORISH PALACE OF THE ALHAMBRA

 1   Plaza de los Aljibes (Square of the Cisterns)
 2   Machuca's Garden
 3   Machuca's Tower
 4   Hall of the Mexuar
 5   Cuarto Dorado (Golden Room)
 6   Courtyard of the Mexuar
 7   Patio de los Arrayanes, or Patio de los Mirtos (Courtyard of the Myrtles)
 8   Sala de la Barca (Hall of the Boat)
 9   Salón de los Embajadores (Hall of the Ambassadors)
10   Torre de Comares
11   Patio de la Reja (Courtyard of the Iron Grille)
12   The Queen's Boudoir
13   The Emperor's Rooms
14   Garden of Lindaraja
15   Balcony of Lindaraja
16   Sala de los Ajimeces (Hall of the Coupled Arched Windows)
17   Sala de las Dos Hermanas (Hall of the Two Sisters)
18   Patio de los Leones (Courtyard of the Lions)
19   Sala de los Reyes (Hall of the Kings)
20   Sala de los Abencerrajes (Hall of the Abencerrages)
21   *Rawda*, or Moorish cemetery
22   Sala de los Mocárabes (Hall of the Stalactites)
23   Palace of Charles V
24   Oratory of the Mexuar
25   Royal Baths

some monuments within the precincts of the city of a thousand towers". In its heyday, when it was the main entrance to the citadel of the Sultans of Granada, it was called *Bib Sharea* (Gate of the Esplanade); later, in the sixteenth century, it became known, with little justification, as the Puerta del Tribunal (Gate of the Law Court) or Puerta de la Ley (Gate of the Law). It is a truly magnificent entrance, worthy of the buildings that lie behind it. As the inscription inside declares, it was built by Yusuf I in 1348; that is to say, at one of the greatest moments of Nasrid art, when the Moslem *alarifes* or architects could create, at the same time, works of disquieting fragility such as the royal Alcázar, refurbished with minute decoration, and works that are solid and strong, almost completely devoid of ornamentation and whose clean lines, broken only by functional openings, possess surprising sternness, force and grandeur. Moreover, the reddish bricks and mortar of the Puerta de la Justicia, either by a most fortunate chance or because of a refined aesthetic decision, blend magnificently with the green shade of the nearby cypresses and laurels, thus forming an utterly harmonious composition. The gateway is set in a large, square flank tower and its walls bear a number of cursive inscriptions praising the glory of Allah and his prophet Mohammed. The heavy structure is worthy of the monarch who built it: " the just warrior Yusuf I, son of the benevolent warrior Abu 'l-Walid ben Nasr", as one of the inscriptions under the archway declares. The inscription continues: " May God make this gate a protecting bastion and enter its construction in the roll of the immortal actions of just men."

The Puerta de la Justicia (*ill.* 59) is 67 feet high and each side of the solid square structure measures 47 feet. Its horse-shoe arch has an open hand sculpted on its keystone; this is the symbol of Moslem Law and may be the reason for its being known as the Gate of Justice. It appears that the five fingers of this symbolic hand represent the fundamental precepts of the Koran: the oneness of God, prayer, fasting, alms-giving and pilgrimage to Mecca. Beyond this first arch there is a vestibule or watch-house which is completely open to the sky for reasons of defence, so that missiles could be aimed downwards at attackers should they manage to capture the gate. On one of the inner walls a vaulted niche has been inserted: this was ordered by the Catholic Kings and it is occupied by a wooden figure of the Virgin Mary with the Christ child in her arms, carved by Roberto Alemán. Beneath the niche there is a carving of the yoke and arrows, emblem of Ferdinand and Isabella. A little beyond, inside the same building, there is another arch with a key carved on it. The meaning of this symbol has long been, and is still, a subject for speculation among experts: according to some, it merely represents the entrance to the city; according to others it stands for the power of opening and closing the gates of paradise that Allah granted Mohammed. The inscription in honour of Yusuf, to which we have already referred, is placed on a marble plaque below a frieze of raised ceramic in pure Persian style, with tiles of green, white and blue predominating. The walls of the inner room of the gateway are lined with stone seats which were no doubt intended for use by the soldiers of the watch. The walls also bear some of the original wooden racks that held the pikes or halberds. Above the gate is an apartment of vaulted rooms reached by way of the parapet, which probably accommodated the keeper of the gate. The gate itself still bears locks and bolts of Arabic origin.

Beyond the haughty Puerta de la Justicia lies the small esplanade after which the gate was once named. This is now the Plaza de los Aljibes, which received

67. Keystone with an open hand symbolizing the five precepts o the Koran, identical to that on the arch of the Puerta de la Justicia. Height 19".

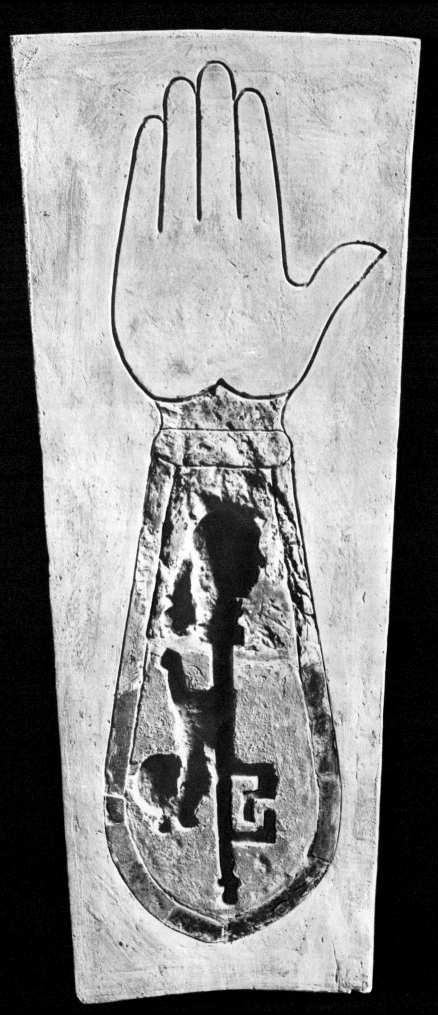

its name from the water cisterns placed there by order of the Count of Tendilla, who was appointed governor by the Catholic Kings and became the first Christian captain of the citadel. On the left side of the square stands the solidly built Alcazaba; on the right the Palace of Charles V and the Moorish palaces; in the background there is a magnificent view over the city below, the gorge of the Darro and the crowded mass of hovels in the Albaicín and the Sacromonte. The present lay-out of this square is rather different from that of the Nasrid period. Then there was only a gully dividing the hill into two, with the Alcazaba on one side and the royal palaces on the other. Later, the governor put in charge of the Alhambra by the Catholic Kings had the cisterns built which were to give the square its name. Soon afterwards, with the planning and execution of the Palace of Charles V, the buildings that once led to the royal Alcázar were demolished in order to clear enough space for a large parade ground.

The cisterns in this esplanade are approximately 112 feet long, 20 feet wide and 26 feet high and are covered by barrel vaults. They lie in two rows which are connected by six sluices. It is now difficult to make out the exact position of the original entrances. On one side of the esplanade, probably close to the site where once stood the Puerta Real, with which it seems to have formed a right angle, is the Puerta del Vino, so called because the space beneath its arch was used to store the wine brought from Alcalá for consumption by the inhabitants of the citadel, who were exempt from every kind of tax. This gate also bears the Koranic symbol of a key and inscriptions in praise of Allah, found throughout the Alhambra. At the centre of the vault within the gate, the Nasrid shield is inscribed with the motto of Mohammed Banu al-Ahmar, " Only God is the conqueror ", amid other stucco work.

The Alcazaba, the oldest building after the Torres Bermejas, rises on the hill to the left. It is clear that below its foundations lie the remains of other pre-Moslem structures, but its present austere and warlike outline was already well known and documented in the eleventh century. Soon after he captured those hills, Mohammed Banu al-Ahmar ordered the construction of some new towers which included the Homenaje, the Quebrada and the Vela. From then onwards, numerous alterations were carried out in the Alcazaba, but its original basic lay-out was never affected. This military enclosure is completely separate from the Alhambra proper, with which it is connected only by the encircling walls. The fortress comprises a large parade ground surrounded by an almost triangular enclosure of high, thick walls and lofty towers. Of these towers the main ones are the Adarguero, the Quebrada, the Homenaje, the Hidalgos, the Pólvora and the famous Torre de la Vela.

The Torre del Homenaje, which has five floors and is about 82 feet high, was fitted out in the sixteenth century as a residence for the governors of the fortress. The Torre de la Vela, once called the Campana, is a place full of historical memories and natural delights. It is more than 85 feet in height and its walls are made of sand, lime, granulated stone and the same iron-bearing clay as that which is found in the walls of almost all the buildings in the Alhambra. On one side of the terrace that surmounts the tower stands a bell-gable with its bell. It was the ringing of this bell that marked the irrigation times for the labourers on the Vega. It is now rung only rarely; in fact, only on the second of January each year, the anniversary of the conquest of the city by the Catholic Kings. To the top of this tower on that day in 1492 came Cardinal Mendoza, the Count of Tendilla, the Master of Santiago and other

68. Elaborate arched window in the Mirador de Lindaraja at the Alhambra, overlooking the Lindaraja gardens.

civic, religious and military dignitaries of the Castilian Court to place on the turrets (which no longer exist) the Cross, the banner of St James and the royal standard of purple, while Ferdinand and Isabella watched from below on the Vega or in the city, their eyes filled with tears of emotion and triumph. It is still said in Granada that the local girls who manage to ring the bell of this tower will soon find husbands—in any case not a difficult task for them even without the bell.

From the Torre de la Vela one can see not only the Alhambra enclosure, filled with light, but also the Generalife and Mount Sol, with their patches of subdued green foliage and pointed cypresses; the valley of the Darro and the Albaicín quarter; the lower part of the city, the Sacromonte and the vast plain beyond; and lastly a long chain of mountains which appear to enclose the whole scene: the Sierra Nevada. Just below the tower, on the spot where the ancient parapet-walks of the Alcazaba were once situated, there is now a magnificent garden and belvedere, where climbing plants completely cover the walls and the flowers and fountains add a unique and delightful liveliness to the scene.

* * *

Leaving the Alcazaba, one crosses the Plaza de los Aljibes, leaving to one side the Palace of Charles V, to enter the Palace of the Alhambra. This concourse of halls, tiny *patios*, miniature gardens and ever-running water-courses, which once formed the royal Alcázar of the Nasrid Sultans, shows what care these monarchs lavished on delightful and pleasure-giving buildings, without much thought of defence and security. Everything in this spot seems to have been arranged for physical recreation and spiritual rest. The imaginative sensuality deriving from the Orient has here created a unique masterpiece of refined and studied voluptuousness. Unlike palaces of the West, this palace has no preconceived plan, no over-all harmonizing concept, for the various halls and the numerous rooms and courtyards were added or inserted in accordance with the growing needs of the Court in the fourteenth century, when most of the buildings that now attract our admiration were constructed and decorated.

The first major surprise in this magnificent palace is that its exterior gives no hint of the beauty of the minute ornamentation of the interior. Its façades are austere and bare, at times to the point of monotony and sternness. This fact seems to imply that the Nasrid Sultans lived more for themselves and their immediate *entourage*, and had no wish for any sort of outward display. This significant detail will recall the idea of the inward-looking character of the people of Granada which we have already mentioned.

It is clear that the Alhambra is architecturally the final effort of an Islamic monarchy already accustomed to co-existence and close contact with Christian peoples and even to vassallage to the Kings of Castile, who for a long time received periodic tributes from the Sultans of Granada. Even when the Nasrid Dynasty was founded, the Arab historians expressed regret at the growing Castilian influence in Granada and at the imitation of Christian customs. As vassals of the Castilian Kings, the Nasrid Sultans were obliged to go to the *Cortes*, which they attended in person, as well as providing soldiers for the military campaigns undertaken by the Castilian monarchs and sending embassies to many

69. The Royal Baths in the Harem at the Alhambra. The star-shaped roof-lights were once covered with red glass.

Court ceremonies. If, in addition to these necessary contacts with the Castilian people, one considers too the inevitable influence that that powerful nation, which had recently conquered most of Andalusia, was to exert on the small Sultanate of Granada, one will not be surprised at the Castilianization of the customs, the fashions and even, to some extent, the psychology of the Moors of Granada that took place from the moment they set up an independent kingdom.

There is no doubt that Christian influence had penetrated the Spanish Moslem world, and this was intensified by intermarriage, trade, and relations between artists, philosophers and writers of the two nations. Clearly, this accounts for the fact that, in the buildings of the Alhambra, the Oriental tradition is blended with some medieval concepts that already foreshadow the Renaissance, although the artists and architects of al-Andalus were still dominated by intensely Arabic philosophical characteristics.

A modern Spanish writer, Prieto-Moreno, who closely studied the buildings of the Alhambra, has put forward a most interesting theory. He asserts that the architecture of the palace possesses a number of concepts that are still valid and indeed fully accepted today, and the principles on which they are based coincide with contemporary ideas. Firstly, the design of this group of palaces corresponds to a human module, where everything is determined by the space occupied by an individual and by his correct dimensions, just as in the Classical ideal of the Greeks. In addition to this first point which has a typically modern basis, we must also consider the integration of the buildings into the natural setting: the scenery and the vegetation are incorporated into the innermost parts of the buildings. The most advanced modern planners can learn a great deal from the open ground-plan, which retains a centre of stability in the use of the *patio*, and the austere shapes and the super-imposed perspectives, which produce effects rather like those of Cubism. In the same way, the architectural style and technique used exhibit a sense of precision, lightness and airiness seldom achieved in any other historical period. The passage of time has shown that this lightness of construction has not prevented the Alhambra from being one of the most long-lasting monuments in history, in spite of the extreme fragility of the materials, which only endured because of the careful way in which they were applied. This is illustrated by the positioning of the marble pavings and the covering of tiles on the plinths that are most exposed to damage by passers-by, in contrast to the situation of the stucco-work, which is placed high on the walls, protected by the eaves when that was considered necessary.

These interesting points made by Prieto-Moreno, which tend to demonstrate the functionalism of Nasrid architecture, can be complemented by the ideas of the Arabist Juan Vernet, which, although they show some differences, are basically quite similar. According to this scholar, the art of the Nasrids was a loyal successor to all the Spanish Moorish art that had existed earlier. It was the enforced isolation of the kingdom that prevented the introduction of new decorative motifs; the motifs that occur were simply selected from the decorative wealth of the twelfth and thirteenth centuries. The floral ornamentation is virtually confined to the use of a single or double long palm, infinitely repeated, and a kind of pointed oval pineapple. The inscriptions undergo a change: the Kufic hand that had been used until then was replaced by the cursive, although this new style retained something of the hieratic quality of the earlier lettering. A popular decorative motif was the polygonal star, which occurs with great

70. Lantern o characteristic Nasrid design.

183

frequency in all possible variations. There is no attempt at originality in the separate panels of the *décor*: every motif is repeated to the point of satiety and even monotony. The exterior of the buildings is austere and devoid of ornamentation, but the interior abounds in sumptuous decoration. The harmony of the designs is complemented by the blending of the colours: the carved stonework is coloured red and dark blue; the mosaics present a great range of shades, from white to blue, green, brown and violet; the carved wood has red, deep blue and gold. Nasrid architecture became structurally weakest with the use of wood and brick only, after carved stone was finally discarded as a building material, except for an occasional piece of marble. But even marble was generally replaced by plaster-work, which was visually effective but lacked structural strength. The over-all plan is typically Moorish: closed blocks containing an interior *patio*, which is surrounded by arcaded corridors on to which the inner rooms open; even the gardens are strictly enclosed. One characteristic of the lay-out is the good use made of the beauty of the natural setting. Being extremely fond of the countryside, the Moorish builders succeeded in harmonizing the fine scenery and the exterior shape of their constructions.

The Moorish royal palace at the Alhambra consists of three independent groups of buildings: the Cuarto Dorado or Mexuar; the Serrallo or Cuarto de Comares; and the Harem or Cuarto de los Leones. The first block was used for administration and justice, the second as the official residence of the sultan, and the third as the private residence of the sultan and his wives and concubines. There are basic differences between these two latter groups: whereas the Cuarto de Comares is clearly Moorish, the Cuarto de los Leones exhibits discrepancies and alien features of Christian origin, which doubtless can be accounted for by the connection between Mohammed V, the Sultan who built the Cuarto de los Leones, and the Castilian King, Pedro I, who restored and furnished the Alcázar of Seville. Such observations as these are not easy to prove because of the difficulty of dating the various parts of the Alhambra; the *décor* was frequently renovated, and many restorations were carried out in the Christian period, first by Morisco artisans, whose work can easily be confused with the original decoration, and then by modern craftsmen, with mechanical perfection, as Gallego Burín points out.

The first focal point in the Moslem royal Alcázar is the Mexuar or Mashuwar, where the sultans, attended by the chief members of their court and family, received their subjects on Monday and Thursday mornings. After a reading of part of the Koran and the acts of the Prophet, the vizier would listen to the pleas and petitions of the people. The poet Ibn Zamrak described this hall in verse in 1365, the year it was completed:

> " Hail, thou welcome, joyful fabric,
> haven of counsel, mercy and favour;
> the handsome moon-like halo of thy form
> is a place of refuge for seekers of justice,
> but a place of retribution for the wicked.
> Thy beautiful cupola, higher than heaven,
> passes from the sight of the mortals below.
> All men are in awe of thy filigreed tissue,
> like the tissue of Spring when the rain falls."

This building, so exaggeratedly described by the " poet of the Alhambra ", exhibits a confusion of styles. It was begun by Banu 'l-Ahmar and underwent

71. Tiled wall in the Royal Baths at the Alhambra.

72. Detail of bas-relief with lions and stags on a trough carved from a block of Macael marble in 1305.

73. Fragment of a Moorish ceramic mosaic.

72

73

74

75

many alterations in the various stages of its construction. Situated in the position that was traditional in all Arabic royal palaces, it was, as we have said, the setting for the sultans' various audiences. The walls are decorated with stucco that may have been made in Seville but which is worthy of comparison with the best work of the Nasrid plaster-moulders. The windows present a view of the Jardín de Machuca, which is named after the designer of the Palace of Charles V in the sixteenth century and which provided a site for the office of works during the construction of that palace. The Mexuar was converted into a Christian chapel in 1632, for which the installation of choir-stalls and a reredos necessitated some excavation of the floor. The reredos was later dismantled and transferred to the Imperial Palace, and the floor was restored to its original level. Leading off this hall there is a small oratory possessing some fine balconies from which the valley of the Darro can be glimpsed.

As we have said, the Mexuar was used for business and judicial purposes by the Nasrid Sultans. It was there that the Royal Council met; there, any member of the public could state his grievances against the civil servants. It became necessary, however, to build a second palace in order to receive foreign emissaries in courtly pomp and splendour. This second palace, now called the Serrallo, was used for all diplomatic occasions, which were numerous since diplomacy was the Sultanate's best means of survival. The third palace, the Harem, was the sultans' private residence. The meaning of the word *harem* has been changed by usage, and much of the original sense has been lost. As Emilio García Gómez declares:

" In spite of the dictionary definition, we scarcely use this word without a slight snigger, as if alluding to an establishment of sensuous pleasure. Nothing could be further from the Arabic meaning. *Harem* comes from *harim*, which means ' a sacred and inviolable place that may not be entered or profaned ', in particular ' the gynaeceum ' or women's quarters. Moslem women must live in seclusion, out of contact with, and even out of sight of, any man, except a close relative. The love-sick wanderer must make do with the sound of a female voice in song or laughter faintly issuing from a latticed window. At most he might catch a glimpse through a swaying curtain of the white hand of a slave-girl holding out a goblet of wine. In this sense, and without making any moralistic judgements, there is nothing so removed from this type of ' inwardness ' as the ' exteriority ' of the lives led by European women today."

For the Arab, beauty is an irresistible incitement, a spur to the mind, which can explain and justify any mad action. Even the prophets could not escape it: Mohammed said, " Any man, while fasting, who looks upon a woman and is able to discern the contours of her body, breaks his fast ". This accounts for the voluminous clothes worn by Moslem women in the street. The early caliphs used to banish or disfigure handsome people. Ascetics would clutch at the sacred veils of the Kaba in Mecca and exclaim, " Have pity, oh God, on lovers and strengthen their hearts ".

*   *   *

The threefold division of the Alhambra Palace was not unique; it also existed in the palaces of Mesopotamia. The arrangement, however, can be best studied

74. Tile from a ceramic mosaic on the wall of the Mirador de Lindaraja at the Alhambra.

75. Oil lamp in wrought bronze. Height 4″; length 6½″.

76. The pool of the Partal and the Torre de las Damas in the Alhambra.

in the Nasrid Palace. Of the three sections, the Mexuar has come down to us least well preserved. Its entrance stands at the far end of a small *patio*, and the main hall, as we have observed, was a Christian chapel from the eighteenth century until a few years ago. The altar consisted of an Italian chimney-piece and an Epiphany painting. In the centre of the room there are four columns, which supported a lantern in the Moslem period and now have a flat canopy of carved wood. Windows were also added, and the ceramic decoration was renewed with tiles made in Seville, which blend well with the original Moorish *décor*. Near this hall, there is a small household oratory, at the front of which is a vaulted niche that faces the *kiblah*, the direction of Mecca, to which the faithful turned at prayer. It will be noted immediately that the plaster-work of this niche has been restored, since this room, together with much of the Mexuar, was damaged by an explosion at a gunpowder factory in the neighbouring parish of San Pedro in 1890. Each of the three palaces has a central *patio*. In the *patio* of the Mexuar (*ill.* 80) there is a central fountain, placed there in recent years, and two sides of the courtyard have richly decorated façades that are very different from each other. The northern façade consists of a portico leading to a much-restored room called the Cuarto Dorado. The portico has a balcony with three bays, supported on pillars with Almohad capitals which are rare in the Alhambra and are probably of Persian origin. A large arch, placed there after the Reconquest, partly screens this façade; it is now planned to demolish this arch.

The southern façade is the finest example of Nasrid architecture, perhaps because it forms part of the Serrallo, or Cuarto de Comares, which was the most important and ostentatious of the Alhambra buildings. Its opulent decoration is composed of ceramics, carved stucco and wood-work. In order to heighten the ornamental effect, the piers are given more emphasis than the bays. The exquisite *décor* of this façade exhibits the chief characteristics of Moslem decoration, which must be properly understood if it is to be enjoyed. In Western art, ornamentation is used to ennoble an already coherent structure: the capitals of the Parthenon columns widen in a delightful curve in order to fit the architrave properly. The underlying principle is nature become art. In Eastern art, decoration is used for its own sake, for ostentation or, as in this façade, to conceal the poverty of a few mud walls. It is the tapestry that covers the bare wall-surfaces. This façade possesses delightful decorative panels, such as the one set between the lower bays and the frieze that fills the space between the upper and lower storeys. All this decoration has three basic elements: the *attawriq* or the stylized representation of foliage; the *lacería* or " carpentry of knots ", composed of ingenious intertwinings of stiff ribbon-carving; and lastly, religious, commemorative or poetic inscriptions, sometimes written in Kufic script, the straight lines of which can be confused with the *lacería*, and at other times in the Neshki hand, which is curved and round. These three motifs are infinitely repeated, not only on the walls, but also in the carpets, fabrics, wood-carving, goldsmiths' work, ceramics and other wares. This occurs as much in Andalusia as in Persia, in Morocco as in Syria, in India as in Egypt. The façade also possesses a fine gable, which is one of the great masterpieces of Moorish carpentry.

The *patio* of the Mexuar leads to the second group of buildings, which is entered by the southern side of the Cuarto de Comares, also known as the Serrallo, the sultan's residence and therefore one of the most interesting parts of the Alhambra. The Cuarto de Comares has an interior façade in which are set two identical lintelled doors, reached by three wide marble steps. The doors are finished with

77. A narrow street in the Albaicín quarter, Granada.

plinths and decorated with tiles, while the remainder of the façade boasts an ornamentation of scagliola and plaster, which must have been coloured in its heyday. It is surmounted by an inscribed wooden frieze and a finely carved gable. The original copper-veneered doors survive to this day.

The left-hand door leads to the Patio de Comares, otherwise known as the Patio de la Alberca and, since the eighteenth century, as the Patio de los Arrayanes (*ill. 45*). It can be claimed that this *patio* is the greatest in the Alhambra because of its proportions and its precise, open plan. It strikes a most felicitous balance between architecture, water and vegetation—a balance that is to be found elsewhere both in the Alhambra and in the city of Granada. Against the white of the marble flagstones the gloomy green of the myrtles stands out, softened by the lighter green of the orange-trees. This vegetation casts a green shade over the still water of the pool, in which the slim colonnades and the richly ornamented spandrels of the arches are reflected. The feature that unites such diverse elements is the gable, which has long projecting corbels that turn upwards, as they do throughout the Arabic Alcázar, and which run along the whole *patio* at the same height from the ground. The high balcony over the colonnade is one of the Alhambra's many fine vantage points for viewing the surrounding scenery.

Beyond the *patio* rises the proud Torre de Comares (*ill. 40*). This tower, which is over 147 feet high, is the highest building in the Alhambra. It is also the most historic, for it was here that the city was delivered up to the Catholic Kings and beneath its walls Boabdil heard his mother Aisha pathetically warning him of the enormous consequences of the treaty he had accepted. Moreover, legend has it that it was in this tower that Christopher Columbus received the gift of Isabella's jewels as a contribution to the expenses of his voyage. In addition, the tower provides us with a view over a scene that is as full of history and legend as the tower itself—all part of the essential spirit of Granada. On top of a nearby hill stand the now shapeless ruins of the Silla del Moro (The Moor's Seat), where the unfortunate Boabdil once took refuge during an internal uprising and looked sadly down on the rebellious city. One can see, too, a ravine popularly known as the " Paso de Lope " (Lope's Pass), along which the Christian armies marched to the plain. Another spot famous in Spanish history can also be descried: the distant row of tiny white houses that once formed the town of Santafé, founded during the siege of Granada by the Catholic Kings, after their encampment had been engulfed by fire. This was the *Real*, or camp, where Columbus was called before the strong-willed Queen and where the treaty that led to the discovery of the New World was ratified. Moreover, the summit of one of the hills that lie along the line of the horizon nearest to the Torre de Comares was the place from which the conquered Boabdil had his last glimpse of Granada, before departing into exile. Because of this the spot became known as El Suspiro del Moro (The Moor's Sigh) in the frontier legends and ballads.

The interior of the tower consists of a spacious hall, which is 37 feet wide and 59½ feet high, and which doubtless contained the *camariyas* or *comerías* (glass panes), from which the tower derives its name. This room is considered as one of the finest examples of medieval domestic architecture. It is also known as the Salón de los Embajadores and once contained the royal throne. In its thick walls are set nine balconies, of which the central one has twin arches with a central column. Above all these balconies there were originally coupled arched windows which were reproduced on coats of arms and engravings of the sixteenth

78. Stucco decoration with *attawriq* designs on a doorway in the Patio de los Leones at the Alhambra.

193

century. The whole of the hall and the other appurtenances of the tower have tiled plinths and above each section of the frieze in the main hall there are five small windows with semicircular arches. The general *décor* possesses the three typical Nasrid motifs: *attawriq* foliage, geometric figures and epigraphy. The hall's present ceiling was placed over the original vaulting and consists of a dome made up of three rows of cedar panels with ornamental knotting, and a square panel of *mocárabes*, on which the original blue and red colouring can be faintly distinguished. These shades, together with the tiles and the other decoration of the walls, must have produced a colour scheme of outstanding beauty.

There is something in the Torre de Comares that confirms the impression that it is the focal point of the Alhambra: in the Salón de los Embajadores there is an inscription that reads " I am the very heart of the palace..." This fine hall is described by Emilio García Gómez, who has a deep knowledge of the Alhambra:

" The vast expanse of wall in this room provided enormous scope for the quenchless decorative fantasy of the plaster-moulders and the *alarifes*. Above the moistened floor of coloured tiles rose the long hooks of the Kufic inscriptions, which were soon filled in with hundreds of escutcheons and thousands of scagliola pineapples and palm leaves. The breaks in this decorative vegetation, which has become yellowed by the autumn of the centuries, contain a network of stiff branches, or else garlands of dry flowers, in which the elegant curves of the Neshki lettering uncoil themselves lazily. Never have any walls been covered in such a complex mesh of calligraphy. All the inscriptions contain an identical message, all the *attawriq* foliage intertwines in the same way, all the arabesques curl upwards in uniform fashion, with the dull monotony of the bars of a cage. Indeed, the Torre de Comares was the cage of Moslem power, which once had flown free across the whole Peninsula. Although the room is rectangular, not cylindrical, it has the same high, narrow proportions and the same finely meshed walls as the cages in which gamekeepers put those plump partridges with their scarlet beaks and feet. The great pool lying between myrtled banks in the adjoining *patio* resembles the drinking-vessel of a cage; the goldfish in its waters are like tiny tongues savouring the sweetness of the sunlight. The dome of the ceiling, made of aromatic wood and dotted with gleaming stars, representing the seven heavens of Islam, recalls the pillows used to prevent cage-birds from injuring their heads against the top of the cage in their desperation to escape."

On the northern side of the Patio de los Arrayanes stands the entrance to the Sala de la Barca (Hall of the Boat) which, according to some, derived its name from the concave shape of its ceiling, although other authorities derive the name from the Arabic word *baraka* (" a blessing "), since this word is inscribed everywhere on its walls. The wooden panelling of this hall, a magnificent example of *lacería* or " carpentry of knots ", was destroyed by the fire of 1890. The Sala de la Barca lies between the portico and the throne room. It was probably an ante-room used by chamberlains, dignitaries and royal bodyguards. Its *décor* must have been exquisite; some traces remain of its murals and of its ceiling-decoration. The splendour that this hall possessed can be judged from the photographs taken before it was damaged by the fire. Its purpose as an antechamber is confirmed by the *alhanías* or alcoves at each end.

Not far away is the mysterious and gloomy Patio de la Reja, where four cypresses heighten the effect of an everflowing fountain. Popular legend has made the railed passageway in this courtyard the setting for many romantic fables. Near

this *patio* is the Jardín de Lindaraja, one of the most poetic places in the Alhambra. Although some visitors consider this garden to be an imitation of the famous gardens of Baghdad or Damascus, it has no Moorish features, being simply a fine example of the European Romantic garden; yet visiting artists and photographers concentrate their attention upon it, rather than upon the truly Arabic parts of the Alhambra. This site was not developed until after the Reconquest. When the Emperor's Rooms were built in the sixteenth century, it was decided to embellish the site, which then formed a new *patio*. The present lay-out of the garden dates from the nineteenth century. As Marino Antequera, the best guide for the Alhambra, tells us, the Moorish gardens were very different in character. There is a famous definition of the Arabic garden by Marçais: " a set of geometric squares imposed on a stretch of virgin woodland ". A fourteenth-century writer, Ibn Luyyun, said that a typical Granada garden in his day consisted of a water-course, a pavilion, an arbour, flowers and trees. In addition, in *Don Quixote* Cervantes mentions the garden of Agi Morato, which was a model for the gardens of the Eastern Maghrib and itself a copy of more Western designs. In this garden there were aromatic herbs and most tempting fruits. The Moorish gardens of Granada, observes Marino Antequera, must have resembled the French *jardin potager* or the English kitchen-garden. In the centre of the Lindaraja Garden stands a fountain with a Western pedestal and an Arabic basin; the latter bears poetic inscriptions on its outer edge.

This garden leads to the Royal Baths (*ill.* 69), which formed part of the Harem. A knowledge of the various sections of the Baths will shed a great deal of light on Moslem domestic life during the Middle Ages. Antequera gives this description:

" As soon as we enter, we are surprised to find ourselves in a room that is as brightly decorated as were all the rooms of the palace in their heyday. The predominating colours are gold, blue, ice-green and red; although this *décor* is not original (having been designed and executed in the nineteenth century), it was the model for all the modern restorations in the Alhambra. This colouring heightens the voluptuous atmosphere of the Moslem baths, which in any case was more pronounced than in the Classical bath. The gay, sporting air of the Roman baths, as well as their importance in social life, seemed to free them of the sensuality typical of the Moslem baths—a sensuality made even more unpleasant by the fact that it took on a certain religious significance among the Arabs. An extant contract, written in *aljamía*, for the construction of a luxurious public bath in Cordoba gives us details of baths in that period. It was to have four sections, with underground lead and copper ducts for hot and cold water; there were to be brass statues of animals with eyes of glass; and the walls were to be studded with silver. The tubs were coated with gold and silver and adorned with inscriptions. The pool received its water from the mouths of metal animals. The ablution rooms were to be richly decorated: the ceilings painted in blue, with silver stars. The total cost was 10,000 doubloons and the work took two years. The building was normally ' cleaned with quicklime, sawdust and brooms ' and illuminated by large wax candles; the floors were covered with rush mats. The establishment was staffed by ' beardless lads ' who provided the bathers, free of charge, with mud, henna, rose-water, and walnut-bark for their teeth.

Since the free public baths were so sumptuous, we can infer how splendid the royal baths, such as those of the Alhambra, must have been. Their appearance now gives us no idea of their former grandeur. On the contrary, we are surprised

81. Detail of stucco and tile decoration in the Salón de los Embajadores at the Alhambra.

82. Fountains at the Generalife by moonlight.

by their austerity, apart from the one room where the restorers have renewed the original gold and multicoloured *décor*. The design of this room is based on the *patio*, an architectural feature that is to be found everywhere in Granada. In the centre of the stone floor stands a small fountain with fine sixteenth-century tiling, which has lost almost all its enamel. This room is commonly known as the Sala de Reposo, a name that suits it perfectly; it is cool and silent and the high windows let in a faint light; everything there induces restfulness. The remainder of the Baths consists of three rooms, which are brightly lit by the star-shaped skylights in the domed ceilings. These rooms are now decorated only by the tiles on the stands, which have been restored. The floors are of white marble, with a central drainage channel. In addition to the cold and hot baths, there was also a steam bath; thus the builders followed the Roman plan, with *frigidarium*, *tepidarium* and *calvarium*. The Baths have a happy, bright appearance that strongly contrasts with the heavy, gloomy air of the rest of the Alhambra. Despite the many changes these Baths underwent in the sixteenth and nineteenth centuries, they constitute the best surviving example of the Moslem bath in Spain. Until the eighteenth century they still contained the huge copper boiler, from which the hot water ran along the pipes set in the floors and walls. It was Yusuf I who built the Baths in the first half of the fourteenth century. Because of their antiquity, and because of the traditional, almost liturgical, importance that the baths had for the Arabs, the arches built there are almost all horse-shoe in shape."

From the Baths, one can gain access to the Peinador, or Tocador, de la Reina (The Queen's Dressing-room or Boudoir) (*ill.* 39), which was thus named at the beginning of the eighteenth century when it was occupied by Queen Isabella of Parma, wife of the first Spanish Bourbon, Philip V (according to other accounts, it was named after the Empress Isabella, wife of Charles V). Here, sleeping accommodation was provided for her and for her ladies. Long before, it had been used by the Moorish sultanas as a *mirador* (balcony for viewing), by which name it is also known. The Peinador consists of two rooms, the Estufa (Conservatory) and another room that is square in shape. A gallery extends along three sides of this tower at the point where the original Arabic lantern windows had been. Both rooms contain impressive paintings by two of Raphael's pupils and faithful imitators: Julio Aquiles, an Italian, and Alessandro Mayner, a Fleming who settled in Italy. These pictures were executed in about 1546, in the style of the grotesques in the loggias of the Vatican, and they are to be found in the entrance gallery and in the upper rooms of the tower. The paintings in the gallery have almost totally faded, but in the ante-room and in the smaller of the main rooms they are in a reasonable state of preservation. The same painters also contributed several scenes of Charles V's expedition to Tunis, which was undertaken to reduce Barbarrossa's power.

Turning back from the Peinador de la Reina, one comes to a suite of six rooms which were called the Habitaciones del Emperador after they had housed Charles V. In 1829, they also accommodated the American writer Washington Irving, who wrote *The Alhambra*. The only sign of the former splendour of these rooms is provided by the ceilings of starred octagons made of unpainted pine-wood, which may have been designed by Pedro de Machuca with obvious Italian inspiration.

These rooms are in that part of the Alhambra that has given rise to most of the fantasies and legends—the Harem, or the private residence of the Nasrid Sultans and their wives, children and concubines. These buildings surround the

83. Panoramic view of Sabika hill and the Alhambra, with the Torre de la Vela on the extreme right and the Sierra Nevada in the background.

83

84

85

very famous Patio de los Leones, to which the Cuarto de los Leones is attached. According to the historian Mármol, the Cuarto contained " the living-rooms, bedrooms and reception rooms where the sultans lived in winter ". It was, of course, the most intimate and secluded part of the Alhambra. The Royal Bath, which had been built earlier, necessitated the placing of the *patio* at right angles to, and to the west of, the earlier courtyard. It thus stands at some distance from the outer wall. As Antequera ingeniously observes, one can easily envisage thousands of women being accommodated in the large harems of Khorsabad or of the early Umayyad Caliphs, or in the vast *hiras* such as the one in Balkh; but here, in this tiny, fragile palace, when we have allowed some space for the male members of the household, what room could there have been for the gynaeceum? Clearly, the many women of the harem, if they really existed, must have lived in the numerous villas and small palaces in the Alhambra village, which has not survived.

In the midst of the Harem, as we have already noted, stands the Patio de los Leones (*ill.* 42). This courtyard is rectangular and measures 93½ feet by 54⅓ feet. In the centre are the twelve famous lions, which are so roughly hewn that they could be taken for spaniels. One citizen of Granada has said that this *patio* is as symbolic of Granada as St Mark's Square is of Venice, as the Piazza della Signoria is of Florence, or as St Peter's Square is of Rome. It is small and quite different from the typical Granada *patio* that we discussed earlier. Like the cloisters of Christian monasteries, it has galleries and pavilions at each end, and in the centre of each pavilion there is a small fountain. This Christian influence has been attributed to the contacts between Mohammed V, who built the *patio*, and King Peter the Cruel, who was called " the Christian Sultan of Seville ". Another *patio* built in the same style and period was to be found in the Albaicín quarter, in the Maristán (Lunatic Asylum), which was demolished in 1843.

Two elegant symmetrical canopies break the monotony of the outline of the Patio de los Leones. But one's attention is centred on the twelve lions that support the fountain, which demonstrate by their primitiveness, contrasting with the elegance of the rest of the palace, the scant development that the representation of animals always had in Arabic art. The original appearance of the *patio* underwent some changes in the course of the centuries. In the nineteenth century the architect Contreras altered the pavilion at the western end by adding a turreted canopy and a cupola of glazed slates. Both these additions have since been removed and replaced by a pyramidal roof. The central fountain of the *patio* once had a water-spout on top of its basin. The removal of this spout to the Parapet Gardens restored the fountain to its original state, as it was envisaged by the archaeologist Valladar and the Arabist Almagro Cárdenas; it is similar in arrangement, as much because of its basin as because of its animals, to the fountain in the Temple of Solomon. The archaic appearance of the lions has caused them to be attributed to the tenth century, but it now seems that they were made at the time the *patio* was built. The twelve-sided basin bears an inscription of a *kasida* or eulogistic poem by Ibn Zamrak, which boasts that the ferocity of these rather stunted lions is only curbed by their respect for the Sultan.

Around this evocative courtyard there are several rooms, one of which is the Sala de las Dos Hermanas (Hall of the Two Sisters). This was the main room of the Sultan's favourite, and because of its excellent condition it was occupied by the Catholic Kings and later by Charles V. Contrary to legend, the name of the hall is derived from the twin stone slabs in its floor, which lie on each side

84. Detail of the tile-work on the walls of the Patio de los Arrayanes in the Alhambra.

85. Another detail of the tile-work in the Patio de los Arrayanes.

of a small central fountain. A magnificent perspective is obtained from the back of this hall through the door leading to the *patio*, with the fountain bathed in the light of the bright Southern sun, which strongly contrasts with the relative gloom of the hall—relative, for over the doors there are windows, and above these soars a marvellously wrought octagonal cupola, admitting the downward rays of the sun. The Sala de las Dos Hermanas is decorated with plaster and tiles, in which violet shades predominate. Above the door leading to the Sala de los Ajimeces is the only original lattice in the whole of the palace.

The Sala de los Ajimeces, or Hall of the Coupled Arched Windows, is oddly named, since it has no such windows, nor is there any sign that it ever had. The ceiling is adorned with *mocárabes* and the hall was greatly renovated in the mid-sixteenth century. The decoration is fine and delicate, matching the eminently feminine character of this part of the palace, which once housed the sultanas. Nearby is the Mirador de Daraja, or de Lindaraja, which opens off a small tower and offers vistas of the garden of the same name. This garden is small and se-cluded and its cypresses rise higher than the windows. It once formed a delight-ful place of recreation for the sultanas. If one were to sit on cushions on the floor of the *mirador*, as was the Moorish custom (this explains why the windows are set so low), one could get an idea of the magnificent panorama that the balcony must have offered before the Emperor's Rooms were built. Its use as a belvedere may explain the name *Daraja*, which possibly comes from the Arabic *ain dar Aisha*, " eye of the house of (the Sultana) Aisha ". This balcony has more connection with the minor arts of the goldsmiths and the ivory craftsmen than with architec-ture proper. Its walls seem to be as chased and enamelled as a fine piece of jewel-lery; parts of the decoration stem from the ivory carving that abounded in Gra-nada in the tenth century. The beauty of the room is heightened by the arches adorned with *mocárabes* and the immaculate tiling of the stone seats, the door-frames and the floor. The arch over the doorway is particularly fine. In addi-tion, there are innumerable carved inscriptions of Ibn Zamrak's verses. The canopy of coloured glass completes the magnificent scene.

One now reaches the Sala de los Abencerrajes, which, quite apart from the web of legend that enshrouds it, is enchanting with its ethereal cupola. Its ori-ginal tiles have been removed, but the room has some capitals that are very pure in style. One cannot avoid being caught up in the ghostly atmosphere of this room, which, according to the people of Granada, is still haunted by the spectres of the thirty-six Moslem horsemen of the Abencerrage tribe, who were put to death there. Although all are agreed on the identity of the victims, that of the sultan who ordered their execution is in doubt—Mohammed X, Abu 'l Hasan Ali and Boabdil have all been named. In the decoration of the room there are signs of the Christian influences that were current at the time of its construction. The domed roof recalls, but does not surpass, that of the Sala de las Dos Her-manas. The hall is lighted by sixteen windows. It is commonly thought that there are bloodstains of the foul deed still to be seen in the room, but these are no more than marks caused by rust.

Nearby is the Salón de los Reyes, which is entered by three large doors, each of which also divides into three, thus breaking the monotony of so vast a surface. The room has connecting doors to several minor rooms, some of which have oval cupolas made of leather-lined wood, and beautifully decorated with motifs that have not yet been fully identified, although they suggest a Western hand, perhaps the work of an artist from Italy (*ill. 48*). In one of these paintings there are some

Carved stucco decoration from Medina Azzahra.

Nasrid figures which may be royal personages, hence the name " Hall of the Kings ". On the other hand, other experts of Arabic art consider these paintings to be authentically Moorish in origin.

This group of buildings formed by the Patio and Cuarto de los Leones is the most compact in the whole palace and is the group that best illustrates the development of the Nasrid style, in contrast with the earlier Moorish styles. Here the various components reach an unsuspected height of sophistication and sensitivity. A new attitude prevails over their grouping and disposition, and the light, colour and water combine to integrate this fragile and subtle architecture, in which the decorative possibilities become exhausted and a naturalistic inspiration enters, contrasting with the more abstract and geometric style of the earlier period. Gallego Burín suggested that the Moors had become weary of the pure line and turned once more to nature, finding there new decorative motifs.

These shrewd observations are complemented by the similar comments of Prieto-Moreno. He asserts that, in the Patio de los Leones, the designers sought to shut out the natural scenery, the sky being marked by the silhouette of the gables and by the rays of light penetrating the plaster open-work of the facings, which give a star-like effect in the interior. The shafts of the columns that form the colonnades, which thicken as they rise from the plinths to the open-work of the arches, suggest the luxuriant vegetation of an oasis, set in a delicate geometric pattern. This courtyard, which was originally filled with plants, bestowed a primitive sense of the closeness of nature on the palace. But the most important element in the *patio* is water, which receives homage in the sense that all the main surrounding halls look towards the central fountain. From the centre of the basin the water gurgles forth like a natural spring, so that when the sultan washed himself there he would experience the illusion of being in the midst of nature. The stalactic architecture of the roofs brings to mind the structure of royal field-tents, pitched before a petrified forest of palms, with a gushing spring at their feet.

Past the Patio de los Leones, in the vicinity of the Torre de Comares, is one of the most peaceful and beautiful spots in the Alhambra: the Patio de los Cipreses, or de la Reja, which was also called the *prado* (meadow) on Machuca's plan. This is a corner full of gentle melancholy and solemn beauty, which has often been depicted by landscape artists. Nearby is the Jardín de Daraja. In this garden there is to be found the entrance to a series of secret passages that lead to the so-called Sala de los Secretos. This name did not come about from any violent political event; rather the room was so named because of the odd acoustic effect produced by its vaulting, which allows a voice to be heard from one corner in another, without its being audible in the middle of the room.

The door of this gloomy underground room leads once more into the bright sunlight of the Jardines del Partal. These gardens have been restored in accordance with the original plans. They are surrounded by interesting buildings which are reflected in the central water-course. These include the Pórtico, or Torre, de las Damas (*ill.* 76), which is fronted by five semicircular arches. Beyond the arches, the doorway has a roof richly decorated in knot motifs, and a room with tiled plinths and several inscriptions. In the *patio* there are also two stone lions, better sculpted than those in the Patio de los Leones. Near the Torre de las Damas, set over a *mihrab*, stands the oratory of the Partal, which has some tiny windows and plaster lattices in its door.

The rest of the Arabic palaces in the Alhambra consist of some towers, which can be visited by following the parapet of the outer wall. These towers include

the Torre del Cadí and the Torre de la Cautiva, where legend has it that Isabel de Solís, the Christian wife of the Sultan Abu 'l Hasan Ali, was incarcerated. It was this same Sultan whose passions led him, it is said, to such lengths as the murder of the Abencerrages. Not far from here is the Torre de las Infantas, which received its name from three enamoured princesses, two of whom fled from their father's court to marry Christian knights then imprisoned in the Torres Bermejas. The legend has been retold by Washington Irving.

In these last mentioned parts of the Alhambra, one can clearly observe the damage caused by the mines placed by Napoleon's retreating grenadiers in 1812. It is said that the attempt to destroy the palace was not completely successful, mainly because of the heroism of a certain José García, an obscure and poor cripple, who risked his life to disconnect the burning fuse. It would be interesting to know from what impulse, from what motives (aesthetic, patriotic or merely military?) this man of the people acted.

Before leaving the Alhambra enclosure, one should look at the Palacio de Carlos V. Really, a consideration of it does not belong here, nor does the palace fit in with the general style of the Arabic plan. The truth is that Charles V, who spent a long time in the city, was genuinely fond of Granada. But he lived in the Alhambra in such discomfort that he decided not to send for his beautiful wife, the Empress Isabella, who was staying at the Monastery of San Jerónimo. Since they had only recently been married, it is not difficult to understand Charles's wish to have his wife with him. In Titian's portrait, the young Queen has a gentle, melancholy expression, perhaps attributable to the fact that she spent most of her life separated from her much-travelled and warring husband. It was, then, a motive of love that brought about this palace; a motive, however, that merely brought to realization the strong inclinations of a prince who had been nurtured in the pompous Burgundian Court and who did not find the austere rooms of the Alhambra much to his liking, requiring a setting more in tune with the ideas of his time. Whereas the Nasrid Sultans, reigning over a diminished kingdom in its decline, had a fine permanent residence in the Alhambra from the fourteenth century onwards, the Castilian monarchs, apart from the virtually Islamized Pedro I, who imitated the Nasrids in his Alcázar in Seville, were constantly journeying through their wide dominions, finding lodging in castles, monasteries and all kinds of modest abodes. At the time when he began to build his palace in the Alhambra, Charles V scarcely possessed palaces worthy of the name, except for those in Madrid and Toledo, which were rambling and tumbledown piles, made up of large numbers of buildings added at different periods and lacking any sort of unity.

The man who was commissioned to construct Charles V's Palace in Granada was Pedro Machuca, a painter turned architect. Machuca was a Toledan nobleman and had painted several altar screens; he had been educated in Renaissance Italy and was a pupil of Michelangelo and Raphael. At the time he was commissioned, he was the squire of the Marquis of Mondéjar, the then governor of the Alhambra, who asked Machuca to design also the Puerta de las Granadas and the Pilar de Carlos V. The work was begun in 1527 and its cost was partly defrayed by the 80,000 ducats that the Moriscos paid annually in exchange for the retention of some of their customs and privileges. This yearly tribute was soon increased by 10,000 ducats, as a result of the building costs.

The palace is a noble renaissance structure, in pure Bramantine style, and if it had been built elsewhere it would have received the fame it deserves. It is

87. Lattice in the Harem of the Alhambra.

square, and has handsome, heavy lines. Its façades consist of two sections, with a bossed lower section. In the centre of the palace, occupying a large part of its site, is the great circular *patio*; the shape and dimensions of this courtyard have led ill-informed tourists to confuse it with a bull-ring. The *patio* is surrounded by a wide colonnade of Doric pillars, while its upper gallery has a breast-work of Ionic columns supporting the entablature. In spite of its incongruous situation, the beauty of this palace cannot be denied. One could say that it is a copy of the best Florentine buildings of the same type. Its grandiose courtyard is eminently suitable in design and situation for the festivals, concerts and public performances of all kinds that are now held there.

Details of architecture: Cupboard in the Salón de los Embajadores, and capitals of columns in the Patio de los Leones, all in the Alhambra. Engraved by F. Giomignani from drawings by Henry Swinburne; 1775.

THE GENERALIFE

The Generalife was the summer residence and park of the Sultans of Granada. Nowhere else does the Nasrid sense of artistry, which, springing from Oriental traditions, has an originality of its own, manifest itself so clearly as in this palace and in these gardens, which are small and perfectly adapted to the soil and climate, filled with sweet-smelling plants, bright flowers, fruits and dense shrubberies, and enlivened by innumerable fountains. The perspectives, as Torres Balbás points out, are not open as in European parks, but distantly glimpsed from high vantage points and windows, which were at one time framed with gaily-coloured plants. Neither in the rooms nor on the paths of the Generalife is there enough room for a crowd. In the avenues and enclosed gardens, two people can scarcely walk side by side. Everything is simple, intimate and in miniature. There is no claim to grandeur, rather, all is hidden and peaceful.

The architecture of the Generalife Palace, despite its perfection, is surpassed by the magnificence of the vegetation. The two pavilions that stand at each end of the Patio de la Ría are half-hidden by the foliage, and in spite of their delicate outline they are subordinated to the composition of the garden. Everything in these rooms and gardens inclines to intimacy, to inner and outer repose. This was the perfect setting for the legend of the Sultan's son, Prince Ahmed al-Kamil, for whom a horoscope forecast a disastrous love affair. The king wanted to save him from this misfortune and decided to imprison him in the Generalife until he came of age. The prince's tutor, an Egyptian sage, was ordered, on pain of death, to educate the prince in all branches of learning, except in the art of love, and to prevent him ever gazing on a feminine face. Everything went well, if a little sadly, until Ahmed's twentieth birthday. Then he fell into a deep melancholy: he would wander alone through the gardens, he scarcely ever spoke, he would frequently fall into ecstasies and softly caress the flowers and birds. One moonlit night he disappeared. No more was heard of him, but he left a note for his father absolving his tutor from all possible blame, and asserting that he had carried out the king's instructions to the letter. He added, " No one is to blame, because in Granada even the silence and the solitude speak of love."

* * *

The Generalife provides a magnificent vantage point over the Alhambra, the city, the Vega and the suburbs on the distant hills. From this spot the kings of Granada could observe the rhythm of daily life in their city with all its happenings; they could listen to the voices of muezzins and watch their warriors marching through the gates of the fortress. The Italian Ambassador Andrea Navaggiero, who spent some years in Granada after its conquest by the Christians, gives an exact and factual description of the Generalife at that time: " it has many *patios*, all of which are well provided with water. One of them in particular is traversed by a channel of running water, edged with extremely fine myrtles and orange-trees. This courtyard also has a gallery, under which are planted myrtle-trees that are so tall that they reach almost to the balconies, and they are so even in height and so thick that when viewed from above they look less like the tops of trees than a green meadow. Water runs throughout the palace, even into the very rooms, making it a most pleasant spot in summer. In addition, in one courtyard that is completely filled with foliage, where a meadow has been made by planting some trees, there is a contrivance of hidden taps by which the water is suddenly turned on, to the surprise of the person in the meadow, and the water springs and gurgles forth, rising to drench him completely. The water can be turned off equally unobtrusively. Above this spot, in another garden, there is a wide, handsome staircase and a small platform, in which a certain flagstone is the source of all the water that runs through the palace. There it is enclosed by many sluices, so that it can be turned on when desired. The staircase is made in such a way that on every so many steps there is a plateau with a central cavity into which the water can be diverted. The stone balustrades on each side of the staircase also have concave stones on top, which act as water-channels."

The outstanding element in the Generalife is water. Water completes it and gives it life; it bestows music and motion on the quiet modesty of the rooms and gardens. Architecturally, the Generalife comprises two small and very simple entrance *patios*, and other larger and more ornamented *patios*, in which the gardens are enclosed by pavilions and walls. It was not, however, the traditional Moorish urge for seclusion alone that caused it to be hidden and enclosed; its situation at a distance from other habitations ensured its safety from prying eyes.

The beauty of the " garden that has no equal ", as Ibn Ammar calls it in his verses—the Generalife, which according to Hernando de Baeza means " the noblest and highest garden of all "—was a byword from the moment of its construction. Al-Khatib praised its leafiness, which kept out the sun; Ibn Zamrak called it " Granada's throne "; and Alonso de Herrera in his *Book of Agriculture*, published in Alcalá de Henares in 1539, alludes to the curious shapes into which myrtles can be trained " if they are planted as those in the Generalife in Granada ". The exact date of the creation of this extraordinary park is not known, but it must have been before 1319, when the Sultan Abu 'l-Walid had several repairs carried out in it and filled its walls with inscriptions. Words are not enough to express the sensation produced by the Generalife: it can only be experienced amid its *patios* and gardens, its gurgling waters and its whispering glades.

* * *

The Koran describes the Islamic paradise as a shaded, leafy garden, refreshed by running water and full of pomegranates and palm-trees, in which " the fortunate

ones will rest in separate pavilions on rugs and cushions of green brocade, surrounded by hosts of houris and heavenly ephebes ". (The presence of the ephebe
was indispensable in most Moslem enjoyments. Even today, the Arabs have a
saying that " goats are useful, women are pleasurable, youths are delightful ".
This Oriental taste appears to have been widespread among the Spanish Moslems.)
These descriptions of the heavenly delights contained in the sacred book of Islam
seem to be foreshadowed in the unsurpassed achievements of the Nasrid monarchs
among the hills of the Generalife.

In this sense, the Arabic garden is a foretaste of paradise, as García Gómez
points out:

" Despite the spiritual exegesis of the theologians, the Moslem paradise is
described in detail in the Koran as a luxuriant garden, which is very dark green
in colour and watered by delightful streams. Moreover, there will be ' fruit-
trees, palms and pomegranates'. Of course, they will not be the same fruit as
the earthly variety, but they will be so similar that the chosen will be able to
say, ' Here are the fruits that nourished us on earth ...' It is well known that
in Islam there is no civil life or laity; religion pervades every sphere of existence.
It is this religious undertone that divides the Arabic garden from the totally
profane Classical park, which Louis XIV inherited from the Medicis and which
they had derived from Rome. Is it possible to imagine a royal pageant being
held in the Generalife, where scarcely any of the paths can accommodate two
people walking side by side? The court of a Bourbon could spread like a fan
amidst groves and fountains, but not the court of a caliph. Islamic royalty has
always preferred to use for state occasions paved esplanades or enclosures covered with chalk—presaging the dryness of the tomb. If a sultan emerges from
his palace nowadays, we see only a green parasol floating over a cloud of dust
along narrow streets that are hemmed in by high, windowless walls. The
Alhambra of the Moorish kings had no trees. The trees were in the moist, silent
gardens, which the king would visit unattended and without his crown.

In this as in so many other matters, Massignon was able to pin-point an
essential distinction. The Western garden is landscaped and tends to overcome
nature; its long, broad avenues cut through the woodland, its vast meres confine
the horizon and its lines of trees stand guard over the whole terrain like soldiers. The Arabic garden is quite different; there, it is not a matter of coloniz-
ation but of limitation; its aim is to seclude rather than to open out, to escape
attention rather than to draw it. There are vistas, of course, but they are
distant and seen from above. Is it an enlargement of the Graeco-Roman courtyard? Perhaps; but that courtyard has been widened to accommodate a fantasy
of vegetation, which is arranged, as we have noted, in accordance with Islamic
aesthetics and even metaphysics. In this respect it resembles a tapestry, with
the greatest possible freedom of frame and line; the lines converge on a central
pavilion, where a dreamer sits in melancholy, though not in sadness, and his
dream hangs on a thread, almost literally, for it is a thread of water. Can one
really grasp what it means to belong to a race, or at least a culture, whose past
consists of hundreds of thirsty generations, who were seldom able to lap up
even the brackish moisture of a well? The legendary Arabia Felix was turned
into a desert by the breaking of a dyke; Roman Mauretania lost its prosperity
because its sluices and water-channels were destroyed. The Arab is aware of
all this and he knows that only the river that flows through Eden never runs low.
He therefore searches constantly for water and when he is successful, he cherishes

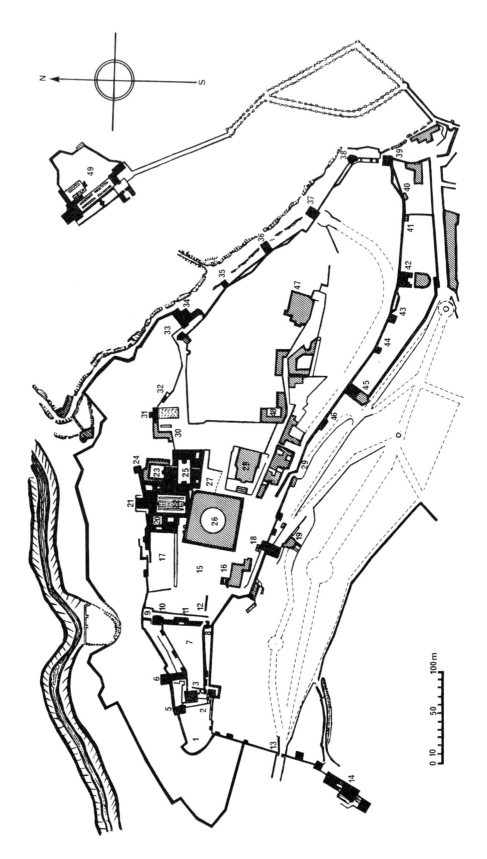

PLAN OF THE ALHAMBRA ENCLOSURE AND FORTRESS

1 Parapet of the Artillery
2 Original entrance to the Alcazaba
3 Baths of the Alcazaba
4 Torre de la Pólvora (Gunpowder Tower)
5 Torre de la Vela (Watch Tower)
6 Torre and Puerta de las Armas (Tower and Gate of the Weapons)
7 Plaza de las Armas (Square of the Weapons)
8 Parapet Gardens
9 The Alhambra Keep
10 Torre del Homenaje (Homage Tower)
11 Torre de la Quebrada (Tower of the Ravine)
12 Modern entrance to the Alcazaba
13 Puerta de las Granadas (Gate of the Pomegranates)
14 Torres Bermejas (Crimson Towers)
15 Plaza de los Aljibes (Square of the Cisterns)
16 Puerta del Vino (Wine Gate)
17 Machuca's Garden
18 Puerta de la Justicia (Gate of Justice)
19 Basin of Charles V
20 Courtyard of the Mexuar
21 Torre de Comares
22 Patio de los Arrayanes (Courtyard of the Myrtles)
23 Garden of Lindaraja
24 The Queen's Boudoir
25 Patio de los Leones (Courtyard of the Lions)
26 Palace of Charles V
27 *Rauda*, or Moorish cemetery
28 Church of St Mary
29 Puerta de los Carros (Gate of the Carts)
30 Gardens of the Partal
31 Torre de las Damas (Ladies' Tower)
32 Oratory of the Partal
33 Torre de los Picos (Tower of the Peaks)
34 Stables
35 Torre del Candil (Tower of the Lamp)
36 Torre de la Cautiva (Tower of the Imprisoned Lady)
37 Torre de las Infantas (Princesses' Tower)
38 Torre del Final de la Carrera (Tower of the Road's End)
39 Torre del Agua (Tower of the Water)
40 Torre de Juan de Arce
41 Torre de Juan de la Cruz
42 Torre and Puerta de los Siete Suelos (Tower and Gate of the Seven Storeys)
43 Torre del Capitán (Captain's Tower)
44 Torre de la Bruja (Witch's Tower)
45 Torre de las Cabezas (Tower of the Heads)
46 Parapet
47 Convent of St Francis
48 Baths of the Calle Real
49 The Generalife

it, channelling it gently between myrtled banks and spraying it playfully upwards from basins adorned with inscribed verses. Has it not been said that the Arabs caress water as the misers in Flemish paintings let streams of gold coins trickle through their fingers? They handle it greedily and fearfully, knowing that the slightest oversight or disturbance may shatter their dream. Beyond and above the Generalife, there were other palaces and gardens; but the water-supply dried up and the oasis reverted to desert. By good fortune, or by some miracle, the water still runs in the Generalife itself. I have walked through all the Alhambra grounds and gone down as far as Jesús del Valle, where the water rises from the Darro and flows silently along a water-channel, stretches of which are encased in clay pipes. Its humble perseverance has an exquisite reward: it bursts forth into waterfalls and fountains, it fills the ponds and nourishes the flowers and trees; its sound reverberates in the woods and over the hills. It will receive its final prize one day, when some great poet attempts to capture the city in a short phrase. In that phrase Granada will not be the fragile Moorish towers nor the haughty Christian structures, nor yet the gardens, but rather the transparent life-blood that courses through its hidden veins and gives it being."

Tile wall decoration.

Genealogical Table of the Nasrid Sultans of Granada

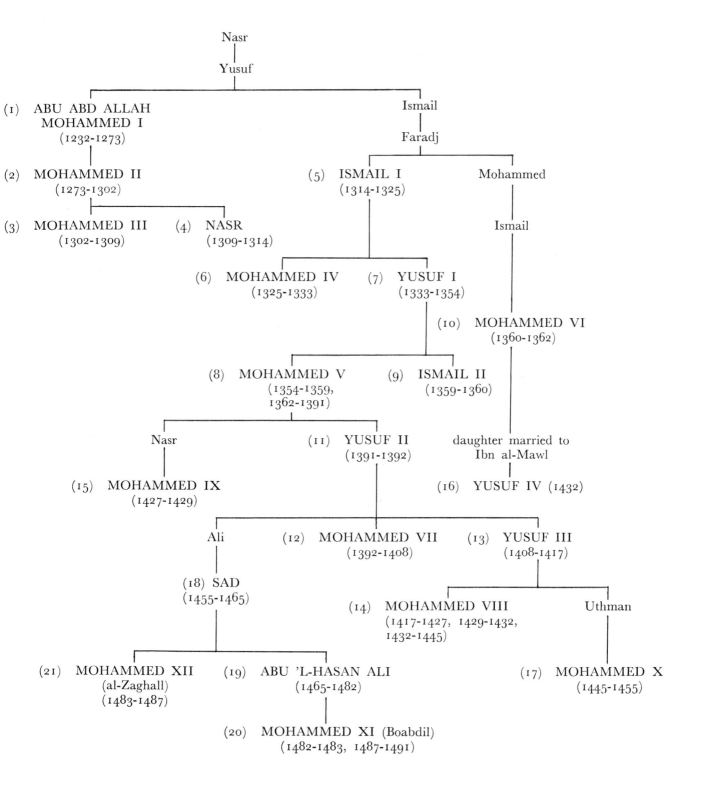

Wall decoration in tile mosaic.

GLOSSARY

alfaquí (or *fakih*). Mohammedan lawyer and theologian

aljamía .... Spanish text written in Arabic characters

al-kasr (or *alcázar*). Moorish fortress or palace

attawriq .... stylized foliage design

áureo .... twelfth-century Spanish gold coin

cachucha .... Andalusian dance in triple time

carmen .... villa (in the province of Granada)

churrigueresco .... Spanish architectural style introduced at the beginning of the eighteenth century by Churriguera and his school

dinar .... Moorish gold coin (minted from the eighth century onwards)

dirhem .... Medieval Arabic coin

fondak .... Moroccan trading inn

han .... travellers' inn in the Levant

manuelino ...... Portuguese architectural style, developed in the reign of Manuel I (1469-1521)

medina .... North African township

mihrab .... the niche in a mosque to which the worshippers turn in prayer

mizcal (or *metical*) . thirteenth-century Spanish Moslem coin of copper and silver alloy

plateresco .... florid Spanish architectural style of the sixteenth century, named after the art of the silversmiths

real .... royal or military encampment

real [*de vellón*] ... an old Spanish coin of silver or of copper and silver alloy, equivalent to 0.25 of a *peseta*

shan .... the outer court of a mosque, containing a fountain for ritual ablutions

suk (or *zoco*) .... Moorish market

tertulia .... social or literary gathering

vega .... fertile plain

zambra .... Morisco or gypsy entertainment with dancing

BIBLIOGRAPHY

ANTEQUERA, Marino, *The Alhambra and the Generalife*, Granada (Suárez) 1960.

BALLESTEROS, Manuel, *Historia de España*, Barcelona (Surco) 1959.

BERTRAND, J.L.F. and PETRIE, Sir Charles, *The History of Spain*, London (Eyre and Spottiswoode) 1952.

BOTTINEAU, Yves, *Spain*, London (Oxford U.P.) 1960.

DOZY, R.P.A., *Spanish Islam: a History of the Moslems in Spain*, London (Chatto and Windus) 1913.

GALLEGO BURÍN, Antonio, *Granada. A Tourist Guide Book*, Granada (Prieto) 1954.

GANIVET, Ángel, *Granada la bella*, Madrid (Libr. Beltrán) 1943.

GARCÍA DE VALDEAVELLANO, Luis, *Historia de España*, Madrid (Occidente) 1952.

GARCÍA GÓMEZ, Emilio, *Silla del Moro y nuevas escenas andaluzas*, Madrid (Occidente) 1954.

GAYA NUÑO, J.A., *Historia del arte español*, Madrid (Plus Ultra) 1957.

IRVING, Washington, *The Alhambra*, London (Putnam) 1832.

LAFFON, Rafael, *Seville*, Barcelona (Noguer: *Guides to Spain*) 1954.

LÉVI-PROVENÇAL, E., *Histoire de l'Espagne musulmane*, Paris (Maisonneuve) 1950-53.

LEWIS, Bernard, *The Arabs in History*, London (Hutchinson) 1950.

MOLINA, Ricardo, *Cordoba*, Barcelona (Noguer: *Guides to Spain*) 1953.

PALENCIA, Ceferino, *España vista por los españoles*, Mexico (Patria) 1961.

PEMÁN, José María, *Andalucía*, Barcelona (Destino) 1958.

PRIETO-MORENO, Francisco, *Granada*, Barcelona (Noguer: *Guides to Spain*) 1957.

SÁNCHEZ-ALBORNOZ, Claudio, *La España musulmana según los autores islamitas y cristianos medievales*, Buenos Aires (El Ateneo) 1960.

SERMET, Jean, *La España del sur*, Barcelona (Juventud) 1958.

TORRES BALBÁS, Leopoldo, *Arte almohade, arte nazarí, arte mudéjar* (*Ars Hispaniae* vol. IV), Madrid (Plus Ultra) 1949.

VERNET, Juan, *Los musulmanes españoles*, Barcelona (Sayma) 1961.

INDEX

221